PROMOTING YOUR BUSINESS WITH FREE (OR ALMOST FREE) PUBLICITY

Books in the "Run Your Own Business" Series

Choosing a Legal Structure for Your Business
0-13-603366-0

Computerizing Your Business
0-13-603374-1

Day-to-Day Business Accounting
0-13-603358-X

Financing Your Business
0-13-603382-2

Managing Your Employees
0-13-603341-5

Promoting Your Business with Free (or Almost Free) Publicity
0-13-603390-3

Promoting Your Business with Free (or Almost Free) Publicity

Donna G. Albrecht

Prentice Hall
Englewood Cliffs, New Jersey 07632

Library of Congress Cataloging-in-Publication Data

Albrecht, Donna G.
    Promoting Your Business with Free (or Almost Free)
Publicity / Donna G. Albrecht.
        p. cm.
    Includes bibliographical references and index.
    ISBN 0-13-603390-3
    1. Industrial publicity. 2. Press releases. 3. Public relations.
4. Small business—Management. I. Title.
HD59.A43   1997
658.8'2—dc21
                                    96-39735
                                    CIP

Printed in the United States of America

Printing 10 9 8 7 6 5 4 3 2 1

PRENTICE HALL
Career & Personal Development
Englewood Cliffs, NJ 07632
A Simon & Schuster Company

ISBN 0-13-603390-3

Prentice-Hall International (UK) Limited, *London*
Prentice-Hall of Australia Pty. Limited, *Sydney*
Prentice-Hall Canada, Inc., *Toronto*
Prentice-Hall Hispanoamericana, S.A., *Mexico*
Prentice-Hall of India Private Limited, *New Delhi*
Prentice-Hall of Japan, Inc., *Tokyo*
Simon & Schuster Asia Pte. Ltd., *Singapore*
Editora Prentice-Hall do Brasil, Ltda., *Rio de Janeiro*

This book is dedicated to its readers, whose entrepreneurial spirit compels them to strive with hard work and creativity to make their dreams of a successful business a reality.

Contents

Introduction

Congratulations on having your own business! There has probably never been a better time to be an entrepreneur. Small businesses are definitely a growth industry. In fact, according to the U.S. Small Business Administration, small businesses are the backbone of the American economy. They create two of every three new jobs, produce 39 percent of the gross national product, and invent more than half the nation's technological innovation. And you have a lot of company as a small business owner—there are now 20 million small companies throughout the United States.

Now that you own a small business, you want it to be a great success—and that means you need to discover ways to help potential customers and clients find you.

Everyone has heard the joke that the only way to get a bank to make a loan is to be someone who doesn't really need it. Sometimes it seems that business promotion works the same way. When you really need to begin promoting your business, you probably don't have the money to pay for it. Yet, the fact that you really want and need effective promotion for your business does not mean that you need to spend a lot of cash.

On one hand, not having deep pockets for promotion probably means that impressive and extensive campaigns are out of the question. An expensive public relations/advertising consultant may be out of your reach.

On the other hand, what you *do* have is your enthusiasm for your business and your willingness to work hard to make it a success.

Believe it or not, that is almost all you really need! Many other business owners have chosen creativity and dedication over throwing money at the problem of business promotion and have achieved excellent results—often better than their friends who were spending small fortunes vainly trying to get the same rewards.

Each of the first nine chapters of this book will explore a different and exciting way you can promote your business. You may have already considered some, like joining organizations where you work together with other businesses. Some may be new to you, like getting the media to notice you or using your computer to profit on-line. In Chapter 10, you will discover new ways to integrate several of the ideas you have chosen to pursue to magnify the positive effects of your work in each area.

Along with the glossary and index, there is a special section at the end of this book that you must not miss. In the Resources section, you will find a comprehensive list of the people whose stories you have read in the book (they are all real people, just like you!) and other special materials that will help you in your business promotion efforts.

Each person listed has shared his or her story in order to help you better promote your business. You might have a question you wish you could ask them about their experience. You might be interested in their business and want to learn more about what they have to offer. The people listed in the resource section have agreed to be there and are hoping to hear from you if you have questions for them.

As you read through this book, do take time to work out the self-survey at the end of each chapter. These brief exercises are designed to help you think and work through your own promotional needs in terms of the concepts introduced in that chapter. If you are borrowing this book from a library, please be kind to the other library patrons and do not write in the book, but instead write on your own paper.

WHAT TO AIM FOR

Because you are so excited about your business, it can be very tempting to take on a lot of promotional activities at once so that you can be sure everyone hears about you. As tempting as that is, it's not a good idea.

Promotional activities are fun and exciting. But you must remember that they are only one facet of your business. As with anything else in life, you need to achieve a balance between the things you want to do and the things you need to do. Be sure you take care of your business while you are promoting it so the new customers and clients you attract will be favorably impressed by their dealings with you.

You might find it helpful to make a time budget for yourself. Like any budget, start with given parameters, in this case, the number of hours per day/week/month, you need to spend at each activity you need to do to support your business. Be sure to include activities like planning, ordering, bookkeeping, on-site management, as well as promotion. Then allocate your promotional hours among the publicity activities in this book that appeal to you most.

For example, if you are a professional in private practice and have twenty hours a month to devote to promotion, you might want to consider writing a monthly column related to your specialty for the local newspaper, attending your Chamber of Commerce meetings, and spending a few hours a month training your employees to be more effective advocates for your practice.

Another example is if you are a small retailer with heavy time requirements at the store that leave about 10 hours a month for promotion. Perhaps you might focus on contributing merchandise to charitable events that will promote your business or giving demonstrations at meetings of organizations made up of people who are your targeted customers.

Even a few hours a month spent on promotion can be highly profitable if you target your activities carefully. Don't rush into anything. Spend a little time thinking about the aspects of business promotion described in this book and which ones you are the most excited about trying. As you get good at them, stretch yourself a little and try something you might not have originally attempted. You might just be surprised at the undiscovered talents you have within you. After all, you started and/or run your own business, right? With some time and energy, you can do almost anything!

BALANCE THE COSTS

The word *free* was used in the title of this book because many of the activities described here require little, if any, cash outlay. However, please remember that there is a cost for everything. (Even a good night's sleep costs you eight hours!)

Be sure to balance (there's that word again) the value of your time against the potential return you hope to achieve from the promotional activity you are planning. You can't always put a dollar value on every activity. For example, later in this book you will read of a person who spent a little time networking over coffee and got a lead that opened the door to contracts worth $1.4 million in 1995. So be sure to time-budget occasionally for the long shots.

As you are deciding on which promotional activities to pursue, don't budget a lot of money for dues in myriad organizations, thinking that membership alone will bring in new business. Most of the time, you need to be able to be active in an organization to reap the maximum benefit of membership. It is more cost effective to pick one or two organizations and be able to participate frequently so that you get to know and be known by the other members rather than just being a name on a membership directory.

GET THE SUPPORT YOU DESERVE

This book is part of the *Run Your Own Business* series. The concept behind this series is that businesspeople, like you, deserve a comprehensive set of volumes that will give them real-life information and skills they can use right away to improve the business they love.

Each book in the series is skill-specific and will give you the help you need to overcome the roadblocks you face today. The first books in the series are targeted at the problems business-people face most. You will find books on computerizing your business, day-to-day business accounting, financing your business, managing your employees, and choosing a legal structure for your business. More books will follow in the next few years. If there is some topic you would especially like to learn more about, please write to me in care of the publisher.

SUCCESS STORIES

One last thought: A real joy of writing a book is learning how people used the information to be more successful. As the author, I would be delighted to hear of your successful promotional activities and how you achieved them. Please send your stories to me in care of the publisher and when I revise this book in a few years, maybe I'll be able to use your story to help teach others!

Now that we've covered all that information, it's time to get busy with the good stuff—promoting *your* business. So, how successful do you want to be? Very? I thought so! Just turn the page, and you're on your way!

1

Working Together with Other Businesses

It has often been said that no person is an island—and it is certainly true that no business is an island either. You need to be aware of the ways that your business is related to others in your community and in your industry.

Your community has a multitude of different ways that it influences and affects the success of your business. Certainly, it contains customers and suppliers. Hopefully, those customers can afford to buy what you are selling and your suppliers can provide you with quality goods and services in a timely manner.

It is helpful if your community is business friendly and the local government actively promotes activities that create jobs and cash flow. It is also helpful if there are ways that business owners can join together to promote the economic health of the community. You can play an important role in making sure all of those things happen.

You may be thinking, "Why should I get involved? It looks like this stuff takes a lot of time and energy." Well, the best reason to get involved is because it is good for your business.

Community involvement will help your business in several areas, including:

- Public image. Being active in community activities will create an image in the public mind of you and your business being concerned about the community and involved in making things better.

- Networking. Other businesspeople are more likely to come to you for their business and professional needs after they get to know you as you work together on community projects and committees.

- Influence decisions. When you are active in community service and business organizations, you have the opportunity to have input that can influence decisions that can help your business. This can range from deciding whether your street gets scarce city landscaping funds to influencing laws that are being considered that would affect your business.

CHAMBER OF COMMERCE

Your local Chamber of Commerce is a remarkable resource that will help you build your business. Properly utilized, your Chamber of Commerce can become a source of information, referrals, customers, and new opportunities.

Each Chamber works to address the concerns of its members and the community they live in. There will be any number of activities you can take advantage of including networking events, social events, educational events, and committees you can participate in to help the business community influence governmental decision makers.

Chambers are known to most people as a place where they can go to get information on the community. Many Chambers develop and keep data about major industries, local resources like hospitals and schools, cultural activities like museums and parks, housing, employment, and other topics of interest to people who might be considering living or doing business in that city. They may even help a city develop an identity that sets it apart and highlights the city's premier business, like "Artichoke Capital of the World." Some cities go for a more humorous moniker that will help people remember them, such as earthquake-prone Coalinga, California's "Coalinga—A City Going Places!"

You will probably find that your Chamber is very pro-business and pro-growth. They tend to work from the premise that a growing business sector leads to a healthy economy. If your business counts on local customers and clients, you may very well find that participation in your local Chamber leads to increased business for you.

"What you put into something is what you get out," states Toni Stewart. She and her partner Betty Walters started Albe Stamp & Engraving in Lakeland, Florida, in 1988. About a year later, they joined the Lakeland Chamber of Commerce and Stewart has been active in many Chamber activities including membership drives, Small Business Week, and the hostess committee that welcomes people.

Stewart says that she has gotten a lot of free publicity as a direct result of her involvement. Just her participation in the hostessing position alone has resulted in her picture, name, and the name of her company being in the newspaper many times. She has found that new customers will mention that they heard of her company before they chose to do business with it and she credits the newspaper exposure with helping build her good public image.

On a more concrete level, Stewart notes that through her Chamber activities, she has gotten to know many other local businesspeople on both a personal and professional level. These relationships have come in handy when she needed to explore business concerns with her banker. Stewart believes that the relationship she had developed with her banker through their joint Chamber activities made it easier for her to achieve the results she wanted in negotiations with the bank.

Your local Chamber of Commerce should be listed in your telephone book or your librarian should have the contact information you need. If you do any business on a local level, you should get in touch with your Chamber and get its membership packet to see how membership can benefit you. There may be benefits available to you that you would find difficult or extremely expensive to get on your own (like health insurance for you and your employees).

The U.S. Chamber of Commerce

You might also want to consider joining the U.S. Chamber of Commerce. This is not the parent organization of local Chambers although many local Chambers belong to it. The U.S. Chamber presents itself as the voice of business in Washington, D.C. It represents business in legislative and regulatory issues and helps its members understand the requirements of legislation such as the Americans with Disabilities Act.

The U.S. Chamber is the world's largest business federation, but that doesn't mean it's too big to work with small businesses. A full eighty-five percent of its members have twenty-five employees or fewer. Along with the Chamber's lobbying efforts, members can take advantage of educational seminars, video instruction, informative brochures, and even a student loan program. The U.S. Chamber's monthly publication, *Nation's Business,* is the largest-circulation monthly business-oriented magazine in the United States. The magazine includes practical how-to advice on many aspects of running a small business.

Depending on the size of your business, suggested annual dues begin at $150 for companies with zero to five employees to $650 for companies with twenty-five employees. All dues are voluntary. For more information, see the Resources section.

If are looking for information about other Chambers of Commerce, referrals to businesses you need to network with in other geographical areas, or information about other cities to which you are considering moving your business, you might want to go on-line to the Consortium for Global Commerce. By going on-line to http://www1.usal.com/~ibnet/cgchp.html you can tap into this useful resource.

Some of the resources you can access on-line include a network of Chambers from around the world, an international business opportunity exchange, merchants and commercial service providers, and newswire and research tools.

PROFESSIONAL ORGANIZATIONS

Especially as a new business owner, you may not yet be aware of all of the different organizations and professional societies that are available to you. You can start learning about them by asking others in similar businesses about the organizations they belong to and the benefits they derive from those memberships. There are also two valuable resource books that you will find at your library.

- *Encyclopedia of Associations* This remarkable resource covers 23,000 organizations across the country. Among the data it includes, you will find an organization's complete name, address, and telephone number; primary official's name and title; purpose, activities, and dues (when applicable); number of regional, state, and local groups; national and international conferences and exhibits; budget information; and official publications, newsletters, journals, and directories. The Encyclopedia is published by Gale Research, Inc. and it is updated annually. If you cannot find it at your local library, you can order it from the publisher (see Resources section).

- *Small Business Sourcebook* This two-volume resource also is a guide to organizations and publications that can help people with businesses ranging from accounting to yogurt shops. Each business listing has subheads such as start-up information, primary associations, directories of educational programs, reference works, sources of supply, trade publications, and trade shows and conventions. This Sourcebook is also published by Gale Research, Inc. and can be purchased (see Resources section) if your library does not carry it.

Keep an eye out for organizations that can help you do business by providing you with information from others outside of your community. These organizations can help you understand how others in your industry are faring in other parts of the country. They can provide networking resources you would never have dreamt of to help you with problems you see in your business. Importantly, you can band together to improve the business climate for everyone in your industry.

Writers and some other professionals often work more on a national level than a local one. Because magazine and book publishers tend to be clustered in urban areas such as New York, Los Angeles, and San Francisco, writers, for example, who are likely to be scattered around the country, may find that a good national writers' organization is more helpful than a local business group.

A good example of this has taken place in recent years. Writers have been fighting to retain the rights to their magazine work as publications began going on-line and selling copies of the authors' work that the publications had only purchased one-time rights to. This meant that the writers, who often sold reprint rights, were finding that other publications were no longer interested in buying material that was already available on-line. It was also unfair for the publications to be selling something (and keeping the money) that they did not have the authors' permission to sell.

Several premier writers' organizations including the American Society of Journalists and Authors and the Authors Guild joined together to fight for their members' rights. The result has been the formation of the Authors Registry, an organization set up to collect and distribute royalties due to writers much like ASCAP (American Society of Composers, Authors, and Publishers) collects royalties on behalf of songwriters. In early 1996, the Authors Registry comprised more than thirty writers' groups and ninety-five literary agencies and had begun collecting royalties.

This is certainly something no one professional writer could have accomplished alone. Also, when most of the members of those writers' organizations joined, they had no idea of how their membership could help protect their professional futures. Whenever possible, you should join at least one professional organization that is national in scope. A wise person once said something to the effect that "Nothing endures but change." Our society and the way it does business are changing at a phenomenal rate. Belonging to a national organization that focuses on your industry will enable you to better understand the forces influencing your business and put you in a better position to deal with them.

Spread Your Wings

There is also a category of professional organizations that is made up of people whose profession is complementary to yours. For instance, if you are an insurance broker, then you will want to be aware of, and possibly active in, organizations for real estate professionals, retailers, or others who need insurance either for their business or for their clients. If you rent linen supplies, you will want to know people in the hospitality industry. If you sell hardware, you would benefit by association with builders, landscapers, plumbers, and so on.

Many organizations have an "associate" level of membership for people in complementary businesses. By becoming an associate member, you have a chance to interact regularly with the very people you are seeking as customers.

There are several ways to find these organizations. One is by looking for listings of organizational meetings either through the business section of your local newspaper or through your local Chamber of Commerce. Most organizations are more than happy to have potential new members come to meetings, and you can attend one or two meetings to get a feel for whether or not this organization is right for you.

Another way is to check with the reference librarian at your local library, college or university library, or business library. He or she normally keeps listings of locally active organizations and has reference books like the books mentioned earlier in this chapter that will be of specific interest to you.

Another great way to find the groups that will have great potential customers for you is to ask your best customers. After all, people like to associate with others who share their challenges and interests. It only makes sense that the people in the organizations where your customers go for networking will be excellent prospects as future customers for you. In addition, attend a meeting with your client and have him or her introduce you to others. The client's endorsement to all these potential clients can be a great door opener for you!

Don't overlook opportunities to be of service to organizations that you might not need to belong to, but that are of interest to the people who are your customers. Professional writer Marcia Yudkin is not a member of the New England Speakers Association, but she has provided valuable service to them, and they, in turn, have been a rich source of new clients for her.

Since 1989, she has attended six of their annual conferences. Yudkin not only helps people with their writing, but also helps them to polish their book proposals and manuscripts for publishers. After each conference she has received a list of all participants that she either added to her general mailing list (so they receive her latest brochure of products and services) or used for a special mailing within a month after the conference. Last year she sent a direct mail piece to the 175 participants on her list and got two new clients!

Yudkin adds, "Every year when I show up at the annual conference, more people recognize me and introduce me to others in the organization. It's clear I've become a personage within the organization even without formally joining."

Barter Makes Good Business

Bartering has been an American tradition since 1626 when Peter Minuit, a director of the Dutch West India Company, traded a reported 60 guilders ($24) in beads to native Indian chiefs for the Island of Manhattan. Today, you can barter your goods and/or services for those offered by others as a handy way to build your business.

Although you can certainly set up barter situations on your own, you may find it more convenient to work through an existing barter organization like BXI (Business Exchange International).

According to Doelle Cecaci, the Diablo Valley Area Director for BXI, bartering is a way to increase your market share, generate new referrals, convert excess inventory, utilize excess capacity, conserve cash, and expand your advertising. You can even enhance employee benefits by bartering your goods and services for products, medical services, vehicle repairs, uniforms, and incentive items.

At BXI, members receive credit whenever their businesses provide goods or services to other exchange members. Participants can then apply those earned credits to the purchase of goods or services from any of the other 20,000 members. Purchases are paid for with a check drawn on their BXI account. All the "banking" is handled at BXI's corporate office. This allows BXI to track all barter activity and mail monthly statements to each member and bill each member a 10 percent cash service fee based on his or her purchases. BXI also handles the paperwork for the IRS and issues members 1099B forms showing their total trade activity for the past year for tax purposes.

Margaret Clark-Mayfield is the owner of MCM Computer Services and a member of BXI. She has traded her computer expertise for everything from office equipment, to meals, and even to hotel rooms at Lake Tahoe for business purposes. In addition she has been able to convert some of her credits to hire a professional photographer for her daughter's wedding!

NEIGHBORHOOD BUSINESS ASSOCIATIONS

Neighborhood business associations are as individual as the communities in which they are based. The associations usually have a definite focus, whether it is individual networking, business promotion, or influencing governmental agencies.

Elite Leads based in Walnut Creek, California, is an example of an organization focusing on networking. Founded in 1991 by Sharyn Abbott, Elite Leads provides an environment in which business people can come on a regular basis to share contacts, give and receive guidance, and improve their skills.

In a fast-paced, one-hour meeting, each of the attendees:

- Does an eight-second introduction of themselves (Abbott says that many members have found that being able to introduce themselves and their businesses quickly has helped them close more deals)
- Talks about upcoming opportunities where they either have something to offer or are looking for something
- Has the opportunity to give "thank you's" to other members who have helped them

- Has the opportunity to mention any special interests they are supporting (for example, charity golf tournaments)
- Does "Power Partner" requests, in which members can mention others who they are trying to meet and see if any other members have access to that person and can arrange the introduction
- Listen to two members do a seven-minute presentation about their business

Obviously, these Elite Leads groups must be kept relatively small in order to get all this done in an hour. Abbott says that groups up to about twenty-four people work well. In her organization, there is only one person per industry in each group so that the focus is on cooperation rather than competition.

This concept has been working so well that she has begun franchising it (see Resources section for contact information).

How is it working for the members? One of the first big successes came from a member who was a public relations professional. She was talking with a person who leased equipment and she didn't think she had anything to offer him when they got together for coffee between regular meetings. But during the conversation, she mentioned a contact who was looking for freeze-drying machinery for flowers that would then be made into permanent arrangements. Her companion contacted that lead and built it into a relationship that was worth $1.4 million in 1995!

Another type of localized networking organization is Women's Network of Contra Costa County. Everyone is welcome to join this organization, although the attendees are usually all female and the emphasis is on cooperation rather than competition. But there are no restrictions on the number of people in any industry who can belong.

Sally J. Nordwall, CLU has been involved with the network for over a decade. In the beginning, she was an employee who was recruiting new employees for her firm and she needed to make connections with other ambitious people.

"I immediately liked it, there was no hidden agenda," says Nordwall. "Everyone was there to promote themselves and their business and everyone was willing to help." Much of her early networking helped her with her then current employer, but as she saw so many other entrepreneurs building successful businesses, a beautiful thought began to blossom in her mind.

The year she was elected president of the Network, Nordwall made the decision to start a business of her own as a financial advisor. She described the decision as "scary and exciting." In early 1990, she made the leap and found that many of the people she had gotten to know through the network, and who respected her skills, were now eager to become her first clients! Nordwall felt that the support she received through this networking organization was crucial to her decision and says, "I don't know of any other organization that would have accomplished the same thing."

If you are interested in finding networking and support organizations that can help you promote yourself and your business, there are several ways to find them:

- Look in the business section of your local newspaper for articles about groups and/or calendars of business group meetings.
- Call your local Chamber of Commerce and ask about networking groups.
- Ask the reference specialist at your library about local networking groups.
- Ask other businesspeople you know about groups they belong to.

Making the Most of Networking

The people who make the most of networking are the ones who do a little planning and practicing before they go to meetings.

Before you go to a business meeting, whether it focuses on networking or whether networking is a side benefit of attendance, spend some time preparing and pay attention to these key tips:

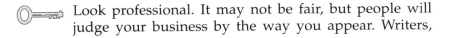 Look professional. It may not be fair, but people will judge your business by the way you appear. Writers,

artists, and public relations professionals often get a lot of leeway on how they dress. Accountants and dentists who dress flamboyantly are likely to be seen as unprofessional.

Have a dynamite opener. Sharyn Abbott estimates that when you are introducing yourself, you only have eight seconds before the other person begins to get distracted by other stimuli. Work out a sentence or two that says who you are and what you do. For example, "Hi (other person's name), I'm Jane Doe and I supply the insurance needs of small retailers." It is always a good idea to use the name of the person you are being introduced to in your statement because everyone loves to hear their own name.

Develop a longer introduction. In meetings where there is formal networking, you will often be given an opportunity to give a one- to three-minute introduction of yourself and your business to either the eight to ten people at your table or the group as a whole. Practice what you will say into a tape recorder and then listen to it. Do you make a strong sales presentation or are you rambling around and not passing on any useful information? Look on this as a one-minute sales presentation and practice until you are satisfied with your skills.

Bring supplies. At the very least, you should have a generous supply of your business cards in a pocket where you can reach them quickly. It looks amateurish to go fishing through a purse or digging through several coat pockets to find your business cards. Also, be sure they are fresh looking. Giving a business card with bent corners and a generally shabby appearance does nothing for you. Depending on your business and the group you are meeting with, you might also want to bring brochures or small advertising specialties to hand out.

Eat before you go. These meetings often include beverages and cocktail snacks. If you try to hold a plate and a glass, and distribute business cards, you'll discover that this is impossible. You'll probably end up making a mess and a bad impression. When you have gone to a number of meetings, you will discover that the movers and shakers are usually moving around and, at most, holding a glass. There is a name for the people who spend most of their time by the buffet table: It is "employees." As an entrepreneurial person, you need to make the most of this time. You'll never know if that extra fifteen minutes you spent at the buffet table (to be sure you got your money's worth from the meeting) will end up costing you thousands of dollars in earnings you'll never generate because you weren't talking to the right people.

 Carry a pen. You are going to need a pen for at least two reasons, and it looks more professional to have one yourself than to borrow one. First, you need to make a note on the back of each business card you receive telling yourself any important points you want to remember from the conversation or any details you need to research for that prospective client/contact. Second, if you have some information someone else wants, you can jot it on the back of your card and give it to him or her. That way the person not only has the information he or she needs, but he or she also has a lasting reminder of the person who gave it to him or her.

After the Meeting

Right after the meeting, sit down for a moment and write a note or postcard to each person you talked to. It may only be as simple as, "Glad to have had a chance to talk with you at the meeting. I'd like to explore ____ that we were talking about further with you. I'll give you a call soon." At the same time, send the person any information you had promised.

Then, before you put those notes in the mailbox, put a reminder on your calendar for a day a week in the future for you to call each person if he or she does not call you first. This is not only an excellent way to prospect for new customers within your community, it is also a wonderful way to develop a reputation as a person who cares about others and follows up on her promises.

A Caution

Now that you are excited about the possibilities that community service offers for promoting your business, a small caution is in order.

Do not let yourself get so involved in doing good things for others that you forget to take care of your business. It won't be much comfort if your business fails but everyone thinks you're a great person. Try to strike a balance in what you do.

One key way to achieve that balance is to set some goals for yourself about what you hope to achieve by working with other businesses. Do you want to:

- Become better known in general?
- Become better known to a certain segment of the population?
- Network with other businesspeople on a neighborhood level?
- Network with other businesspeople on a community-wide level?
- Create reciprocal relationships with other businesspeople?
- Increase your stature within your industry?

Once you decide what you hope to achieve through your professional involvement, you will be better able to decide which activities are most likely to help you.

There is one last thing to keep in mind. Although it is important to have goals you hope to achieve by working with other businesses, you also need to be willing sometimes to work for the good of the community or the organization even if you do not see any immediate benefit to yourself.

It is a strange but true fact that by helping others you really do help yourself. Or as some people say it, "What goes around, comes around." If you only seem interested in your own profit, other people will notice and it will have a negative impact on your life and your business. However, if you participate in organizations in a way that promotes your whole industry or community (see Chapter 2) and the other people and businesses in it, you will undoubtedly be amazed at the long-term benefits that accrue to you.

SELF-SURVEY: WORKSHEET FOR EVALUATING BUSINESS/PROFESSIONAL AFFILIATIONS

Local Organizations	Contact Name/ Telephone Number	Date Called
_____	_____	_____
_____	_____	_____
_____	_____	_____
_____	_____	_____
_____	_____	_____

State/National Organizations	Contact Name/ Telephone Number	Date Called
_____	_____	_____
_____	_____	_____
_____	_____	_____
_____	_____	_____

Groups I Decided to Visit:

Group: _____

Date: _____

Impression of its usefulness: _____

_____

Group: _____ Date: _____

Impression of its usefulness: _____

_____

Group: _____ Date: _____

Impression of its usefulness: _____

_____

Groups I Decided to Join:

Group: _____ Date: _____

Group: _____ Date: _____

2

Achieving Great Benefits by Doing Good

Everybody loves a hero, and that is just what you can become by helping out others in need. Depending on your business goals, you may choose to help at a neighborhood or community level or even at a national level. You can be active in organizations that relate directly to your business, or you can choose to be active in non-business-related activities where the positive name recognition will be your primary business benefit (but never overlook the pure satisfaction of helping other people primarily as a personal benefit).

Whether you are working with charities, local service organizations, or schools, you need to realize that they have their own bureaucracies and their own needs. The most successful relationships you develop in this arena will be the ones in which you recognize their needs and work with them to form a mutually beneficial relationship. Unfortunately, a few people try to force organizations to do events solely on the "volunteer's" terms, and these rarely result in the good will and good promotion that the people who started them had envisioned.

WORKING WITH CHARITIES

By their very nature, charities seem to always be looking for one more sponsor or one more good fund-raising event. Once you get known as someone who volunteers, you will be approached by many people who want you to be active in or contribute to their favorite cause.

So before you look for a charity to help, it makes sense to decide what you want from your participation and what you are willing to do to achieve that goal. For instance, if you sell medical supplies or provide physical therapy, you might choose to affiliate with a health-oriented charity. If you own a nursery or design gardens, you might want to be active in refurbishing parks or landscaping historical sites. If you run a print shop, you might want to be active in local political campaigns. If you sell insurance, you might want to be active in fire prevention programs or charities that work to prevent drunk driving. If you are a builder or in building supply sales, you might want to get involved with a Habitat for Humanity project. As you can see, the kinds of organizations you can join and the ways they can relate to your business are only limited by your imagination.

There is one more thing to consider. There may be times you, a family member, or an employee were touched by a problem a charity is working to fix, or were helped by a charity. This can be an excellent reason for choosing a particular charity. Even if you don't immediately see how you will benefit from the association, give it a try. Sometimes the most beneficial relationships come from the most unexpected places.

Having said that, if you don't have a charity you feel especially motivated to assist, a good way to start your charitable activities is to decide what you hope to get from them.

GOALS I WANT TO ACHIEVE

☐ Increased name recognition for my business

☐ Recognition for being associated with a particular cause

Name of cause _____

☐ Association in the public mind between my products/services and the needs of the charity's beneficiaries

☐ Networking with others associated with the charity

☐ Potential tax benefits

☐ Giving back to my community

☐ Other: _____

_____

_____

_____

WHAT I'M WILLING TO DO TO ACHIEVE MY GOALS

☐ Donate $_____ per _____

☐ Donate products/services worth $____ per _____

☐ Give _____ hours of my time per _____

☐ Work related to my business

☐ Work suggested by the charity but not business-related

☐ Group activities

☐ Solitary activities

☐ Other talents I have to share _____

_____

_____

☐ Attend meetings

☐ Bring in other business associates/friends to help

☐ Other _____

_____

_____

_____

Approaching a Charity

You can approach a charity either by telephone or letter, whichever you are most comfortable with. Tell them who you are and (if you've already decided) what you have to offer. Ask the charity's representative what it needs.

For instance, if you are approaching a Muscular Dystrophy Association regional office in the early summer, it is gearing up for its Labor Day Telethon and the Association may need anything from people to sponsor and/or work events leading up to the Telethon to people to sponsor and/or work the Telethon itself. A great side benefit of this is that depending on your level of help or donation, you may be able to have your company listed or even introduced on the regional Telethon telecast.

Getting the Credit You Deserve

One of the great things about helping charities is that they often are generous with their gratitude. They may give recognition by listing your name and/or your business on programs or mentioning it during introductions at events or by giving certificates suitable for framing or even trophies or plaques.

The listings and introductions can be a wonderful way to acquaint potential new customers with your business. People who are active in a charity will often go out of their way to do business with people who support their cause. Others who hear or read of your activities may decide to do business with you to support someone who is so community-minded.

The trophies and plaques serve another purpose. Aside from the potential new customers who see you receive them, they are something you can display in your business to let your current customers know that you help others.

There is also the hidden benefit that is not exactly a "credit," but does have the ability to help you. Whenever you work with a charitable organization, you will meet new people and have the potential to network with other businesses that could prove of value to you. As was mentioned earlier, when you do this, you never know what fascinating people you will meet and what unexpected rewards will come your way.

COMMUNITY SERVICE CAN SERVE YOUR BUSINESS

Community service certainly can include helping charities, but it also covers a wide range of other opportunities for you to get involved with and benefit from organizations and activities right where you do business.

One opportunity you should not overlook is the local service clubs like Lions, Rotary, Kiwanis, and Elks. Although they do not have as strong a business tie-in as the professional organizations discussed in Chapter 1, they are excellent ways to meet other people who are active in your community. These clubs usually have monthly meal-time meetings and often include a program (maybe you could even be a speaker!). You will make new friends while you establish yourself and your company as being concerned about local people and needs.

These service clubs usually do more than just have meetings. They are active with all sorts of activities in the community. Try to get in on the planning committee for upcoming events and you will have the opportunity to get the work assignments that best suit your talent and your business resources.

Consider the needs of cultural organizations in your community. Your business may have an affinity with libraries, musical organizations such as symphonies, theater groups, museums for everything from art to military history, or even zoos. If so, you could benefit from your association with the groups that support those organizations.

One relatively new opportunity to combine your company's ability to do community service with your promotional needs is to "adopt" a section of a highway. In many areas, the governmental bodies that maintain the roads will allow a business to do this and will place a sign with your business name on it along the highway. In return, you must clean up the roadside litter along your stretch of adopted highway. Other areas that have problems with graffiti on walls will allow businesses to adopt a wall and paint over graffiti when it appears. Usually when you do this, a sign is posted prominently telling all motorists that you perform this pubic service. You can incorporate this into your efforts to build team spirit by having a picnic or pizza party following each clean-up party. Call the governmental body responsible for road maintenance in your area to find out if it has this kind of program and what the requirements are.

Community organizations also include some of the younger members of society. Depending on your company and your talents, you could become involved with youth activities like Scouts, 4-H, sports teams, etc. There are a lot of ways you can be of service to youth groups for very little or no money, such as offering field trips to your business, giving demonstrations of what you do or sell, giving talks about topics involved in your work that they can relate to, or allowing them to use a room in your business for meetings. If you have some money to invest in the next generation, consider sponsoring a sports team or being involved with other groups a little more deeply. Anything you do for children will pay big dividends for you personally and in building public appreciation for your business.

Finally, when you are considering community service opportunities, be sure to consider opportunities related to religious organizations. These organizations can be doing events that vary in size from small projects such as food pantries or rummage sales to major projects that affect the whole community. As discussed earlier, you should evaluate any potential commitment based on many factors. You should ask yourself:

- Will this particular activity enable me to meet potential customers/clients?
- Will I make important business-to-business contacts here?
- Will this activity offer me any potential media coverage?
- Am I able to commit the time or money it requires right now?
- Is this something that will give me personal satisfaction?

Like your work with charities, schools, and professional organizations, working with community service groups will benefit your business at several levels including name recognition, networking, and direct contacts with people who can become new customers and clients (not to mention the other people they tell about you).

Remember that your employees are also great ambassadors for your business. If you do not have the time to get involved with all the organizations that would help your business, one way to maximize the benefits of being part of community organizations is to support your employees who want to be involved with these groups. Your support can be as simple as allowing them a longer lunch hour on meeting days so they can attend, or helping them pay dues.

One more thing to remember is that under some circumstances, costs incurred because of business involvement with community service organizations may be tax deductible. Talk with your business tax advisor to see how you could save money because of your good deeds.

Don't Overlook the Larger Community

There can be times when you and your business can benefit from reaching out beyond your local community to give service in ways that will benefit yourself and many others. Keep an eye out for those opportunities; they may appear in the most surprising places.

You might not think that someone running a small business in the picturesque town of Winona, Minnesota could have much of an influence on national governmental policy on small businesses. Just don't tell that to Carol Jensen! Jensen is the owner of Jensen Business Development and she was one of twenty delegates elected from a field of nearly 300 businesspeople to represent Minnesota at President Clinton's White House Conference on Small Business held in June 1995. Professionally, Jensen helps other small business owners with their business plans, start-ups, strategic marketing, and financial analysis. Because of this, she is exceptionally knowledgeable about the roadblocks that people face when they are trying to get their new businesses up and profitable.

Her delegation met monthly for about six months to study a priority list and research and develop issues they wanted to bring attention to at the conference. Her special issue was promoting business ownership as a career option. She found that only sixteen high schools in the entire nation and approximately ninety universities offered programs that teach young people how to become entrepreneurs.

Jensen had a wonderful time at the conference and served on the Implementation Committee for her region. She hopes that the work done by everyone there will result in some substantial assistance for small business owners and employees. In all probability, she will see her work affect future legislation. After all, at the 1986 conference, sixty recommendations were made and twenty-three of them have already become laws!

While not everyone can attend a White House conference, you can keep an eye out for unique opportunities that will allow you to both strengthen your business and serve others.

SUGGESTED IDEAS FOR COMMUNITY ACTIVITIES FOR BUSINESSPEOPLE

Here are some typical small business careers as well as suggestions about different kinds of volunteer service opportunities these owners are likely to find. When you read this, consider your own career and try to come up with ways you can help others.

If you are a:	You can:
plumber, carpenter, or electrician	help Habitat for Humanity or other groups that build and rehabilitate housing for low-income families, teach simple home repair skills at senior centers
attorney	work pro bono for local agencies, teach consumer law to high school students
therapist	teach volunteers at a crisis hot line, work with groups that help troubled teens or people doing caregiving for family members with Alzheimer's disease
florist	arrange flowers for charitable events, teach flower arranging to youth groups
manufacturer	give tours to educate youth, offer product to organizations for fundraisers

chef or restaurant owner	donate food for charity events, teach cooking skills and nutrition to school students
your profession	_____

THE A-B-C'S OF WORKING WITH SCHOOLS

Today schools often are in very real need of assistance from the people and businesses in their communities. By helping out, you create goodwill among the very people (teachers, parents, students, and even people who read about how you helped the school in newspaper articles) who can make excellent customers for your business.

The type of activities you engage in with a school will depend on its needs and your resources. Many activities will be relatively low cost or even free. A few might even show a profit for you as you help the school. For instance, if you have a bookstore, you might arrange with a Parents' Club to have a book sale on campus and you will donate a certain percentage of the gross receipts to the club as a credit toward purchasing books from you for classrooms or the school library.

A low-cost option for a landscaper or nursery owner is to work with a class or two to beautify an area of the campus. The local newspaper would probably be interested in taking photos and doing a short article about the activity, which would be great free publicity for you. You also could supply discount certificates to the school, which students could take home to their parents. Those parents would be likely to use them to show their support for your help at the school.

Keep an eye open for the times when schools offer relatively low-cost, no-work ways to help out. School newspapers and yearbooks often sell advertisement space at a very reasonable price. There may be seasonal activities in which they solicit contributions of money or merchandise for everything from school plays to Halloween carnivals to safe and sober graduation parties. Programs are often handed out at these events to attendees, and your business will be listed as a donor.

Remember that not everything you do has to have a direct, measurable business benefit. Any time you help improve the quality of education that is available to local students, you are also helping to raise the quality of the future employees that will be available to you and other businesspeople in your community. It can also be personally satisfying to know that your efforts have made life more pleasant, interesting, or rewarding for young people where you live and do business.

Getting Involved

There are several ways to choose a school to work with. Pick the ones that suit you best. You may want to choose a school that:

- Your kids or your employees' kids attend.
- Offers educational opportunities that are related to your business. For example, if you have an auto repair shop, you would look for a high school that offers an auto shop class.
- Has students who are likely to be especially interested in your business. For example, if you sell musical instruments, you would be interested in working with schools that have children who are ready to begin instrumental music training.

When you have targeted one or more schools you would be especially interested in working with, contact each school's principal and explain that you would like to help and what you have to offer (such as the ability to give a presentation, tutor students, or provide a service). Also ask what the school needs because it may have a need you could fill that you didn't think of.

Remember that while you may get promotional benefits in terms of listings in programs or other obvious ways, you will also have the benefit of increased name recognition and the goodwill that results from people associating you with the school's activities.

Achieving the Maximum Benefit

Whichever community support activities you choose to become involved in—and even if it is primarily because you see a job that needs to be done, not because your only interest is promoting yourself or your business—it never hurts to keep an eye out for the best ways to get some publicity.

A favorite way to keep people aware of your contribution is by giving T-shirts or caps. In one early promotional concert, Hawaiian Tropic tanning products gave promotional T-shirts to the people who were helping the band, and those shirts immediately were in great demand. Not only were they popular, every time one of the workers was seen in the shirt, he or she was a walking billboard for Hawaiian Tropic.

Think of the possibilities. If you and your employees are helping to clean up a park or renovate a home for an elderly person, matching company T-shirts will make you all stand out in the crowd and everyone will notice. You also may be fortunate enough that any news photographers there will take pictures that include people wearing your shirts, giving you extra free publicity.

There is another option to consider if you have a little money to invest. If you provide the shirts for some local event, such as a charity 10-K race, with the name of the event on the front and your company logo on the back, you will also be getting free publicity every time someone wears his or her shirt for the next few years.

Chapters 1 and 2 concentrated on working with other people and organizations. These activities are wonderful, but you will normally not have a lot of control over them unless you are in charge. In the next seven chapters, you will learn exciting ways to promote your business that you can take charge of yourself. You also will discover promotional activities you can use, such as public speaking, with your charitable efforts. So keep the ideas you have been contemplating in mind as you continue with the book. But first, spend a few minutes and do the Self-Survey sheet on the next page.

SELF-SURVEY: WORKSHEET FOR CREATING GOODWILL THROUGH SERVICE

Charity I want to contact: _____

What I have to offer them: _____

Date contacted: _____

Person spoken to: _____

Its needs I may be able to fill: _____

_____

Action taken: _____

Benefit I expect to receive: _____

Community service organization I am considering becoming involved with: _____

Date visited meeting: _____

Contact person: _____

Types of service opportunities this organization offers: _____

Specific service opportunities that best suit my business's needs and resources: _____

_____

Action taken: _____

Benefit I expect to receive: _____

Schools I am considering becoming involved with: _____

_____

What I have to offer: _____

Date contacted: _____

Person spoken to: _____

Their needs I may be able to fill: _____

Action taken: _____

Benefit I expect to receive: _____

3

Fun, Fun, Fun

While promoting your business is certainly hard work, no one ever said you couldn't have some fun while you were doing it!

Sometimes everyone gets so caught up in the serious work of doing business, that they forget how much they planned to enjoy that venture when they started it. How about you? Have you been having some fun while you manage and promote your business?

This chapter is dedicated to the proposition that you can develop promotions for your business that will be fun for you and your customers. People like to enjoy themselves. When you make it possible for them to connect your business and their pleasure in their minds, you have created a very positive connection.

In this chapter you will explore three exciting ways businesses can bring fun into their promotions. You may be able to use one or more of these ideas right away. You might need to let others simmer in the back of your mind for a while until you come up with just the right approach that will attract the customers you want.

Also, as you think about your whole promotion plan, consider ways that you can add some of these fun concepts to other promotional activities in order to build customer interest.

CREATING WINNING CONTESTS

There is an element of fun in any contest, but you want to be sure that there is a business benefit for you in any contest you sponsor. The cost does not have to be significant, but the contest has to appeal to the people who would make good customers and clients for you. Equally important, these people must feel there is a value to them to enter your contest.

In his book, *Guerrilla Marketing Weapons,* best-selling author Jan Conrad Levinson states that there are five main reasons for businesspeople to have contests. They are to:

1. Have people try your product or service.
2. Make people aware of your product or service.
3. Show people how to get to where you sell.
4. Get names for your mailing list.
5. Gain free publicity.

Another reason you could certainly add to the list is to "create goodwill in the community," because people like to do business with others who care about the city where they live and work. And contests that recognize the accomplishments of people in the community are sure winners themselves.

Creating a Simple Contest

One of the most simple and economical contests is a coloring competition. Real estate professional Bev Marshall, with the C.C. Connection office of ReMax in Walnut Creek, California, estimates that she spends approximately $30 each Halloween making fliers with a seasonal picture for entrants to color (most entrants are kids, but she has had people up to 61 years old enter). She delivers approximately 500 copies to homes in the neighborhoods where she focuses her business.

Her only other cost is approximately $1.50 each for a seasonal novelty toy for each winner—and each entrant is a winner, of course. She feels that this contest, and other similar efforts she does about every other month, help keep her name in front of her target clients and build goodwill. In fact, Marshall says that 95 percent of her business comes from the areas where she actively promotes herself.

What other kinds of contests might interest you? How about:

- A drawing. Prizes might be
  - a turkey or ham near the holidays
  - a service you offer professionally
  - a product you normally sell
  - an item that is hard to acquire but in high demand (for example, sometimes shortages occur for popular toys)
  - tickets to a sporting event
  - opportunity to meet a celebrity you have access to
  - a meal at a local restaurant
  - a chance to appear in a radio or television commercial you are planning
- A skill contest (related to your business). Good prizes might be merchandise or gift certificates. Think about holding:
  - 5K and 10K races if you own a store that sells running shoes
  - an art show if you sell art supplies or do framing
  - a chili cook-off if you sell food or kitchen supplies
  - a fashion show if you sell clothes or sewing items

Choosing Winning Prizes

Certainly, some of the prizes mentioned earlier could entail some costs. However, before you buy them, consider contacting the sports team or toy manufacturer, etc. and trying to arrange to have them donate the item in exchange for the exposure your contest will give them. If the prizes are merchandise from your store, a supplier might want to donate the prizes in exchange for cosponsor status at the event.

When you are deciding on a prize, be sure that it will have benefit to the typical customers you want to attract. If your prize is something they can use only if they purchase something else from you, they may feel that it is worse than no prize at all, and that will only gain you ill will. Also, some prizes, like live animals, may make for great photo opportunities when they are presented, however, it would be highly irresponsible to award a pet to someone who was not prepared to properly care for it.

Designing an Effective Entry Form

Everyone will agree that an effective entry form includes a place for entrants to write their names, addresses, and telephone numbers so you can contact the winner easily. Be sure to make the form large enough to allow people to write or print clearly. If you leave a one inch line for the street address, and an entrant has a long address (they may live on a street with a long name and in an apartment), they may not be able to write legibly.

Hawaiian Tropic vice president Jack "Corky" Surrette notes that you also might want to think about including a statement on the entry forms limiting people to one entry per person.

Back in 1976, he was a distributor for the then relatively new Hawaiian Tropic tanning and skin care products. For months, he had successfully displayed a Hobie 12 Monocat boat (in shopping centers, on beaches, etc.) that was to be given to the person who came closest to guessing the exact number of people who attended a special 4th of July concert. The boat, with "Hawaiian Tropic" boldly emblazoned across the sail, had attracted a lot of attention so there had been thousands of entries. However, there was no notice on the entry form limiting the number of times a person could enter.

One man who apparently desperately wanted the prize arrived before the close of the entries with a companion and boxes of entries he had duplicated, each with a different estimated attendance. Not surprisingly, he won. If you want to prevent this kind of participation in your contest, be sure to place a statement in the rules limiting the number of entries per person or address.

Getting Full Value

When you have offered a contest, don't throw away all the losing entries or you may be throwing away a great deal of potential business. Remember, through your efforts, all these people have gained new knowledge of your business and what you might have to offer them. They each took the time to fill in your entry forms—giving you their names and contact information.

If you were clever you also asked one or more other questions on the entry form to help you determine whether they might be interested in your goods or services in the near future. For instance, a real estate professional might ask questions like "Do you plan to move in the next six months?" or "Would you like a no-cost evaluation of your home's current market value?"

Positive answers to these kinds of questions mean that these people are prospects that you want to get in touch with as soon as possible. Even entry forms that just have names and addresses can be used to develop a computerized database for sending future mailings, because you know they have already noticed your business.

WHEN SHOULD YOU *ENTER* CONTESTS?

There is another side of contests that you should definitely keep in mind—entering them. No, not the lottery.

Winning contests related to your business can be an opportunity for wonderful publicity. The immediate benefits can include write-ups about your accomplishment in everything from local newspapers to national trade magazines. If there is something extraordinary about your entry or the award, local television programs may even be interested in doing a segment on it. The long-term benefits can be achieved by displaying your award at your place of business. Seeing award certificates and trophies in your business shows your customers and clients that your expertise has been recognized and rewarded by your peers.

Where Do You Find These Contests?

Start looking for contests by really reading the magazines you subscribe to that are targeting people in your business. Many of them have annual contests. (Hint: The contests may not be advertised every month, you may need to look back over a year's worth of magazines to find them.)

Other excellent places to find prestigious contests are professional organizations you belong to. The competitions they sponsor are likely to be written up in the newsletter or magazines you receive from them.

Once you have developed a list of contests you are interested in entering, rank them in order of how well they will help you achieve your promotional goals. For instance, if your primary goal is to get investors interested in helping you franchise your business, then national awards in your industry are more likely to be impressive than an award from your neighborhood business association.

There are likely to be some costs associated with entering contests. First, do not forget the value of your time. It can take anywhere from a few hours to a few days to fully prepare a contest entry. You'll want to do your best work to give yourself the best possible chance of winning.

There may also be expenses for photography of your entry. This is no place to be too budget-minded. A bad photograph can give a bad impression of even the best project, so if you are not a professional photographer, consider hiring one. The cost may be relatively minimal if the contest is about jewelry you designed or some other small object that can be taken to the photographer's studio. If you are an architect, landscape designer, or interior decorator, the photographer will have to come to your project. In these cases, be sure you get a photographer who specializes in architectural photos as it takes special expertise to get the lighting right in these kinds of pictures.

While the "sitting" fee for having photography done may be somewhat expensive, the more uses you can find for the photos, the less your actual cost per use.

Think about multiple uses for the photographs. First, you may be able to use the same photos to enter multiple contests unless some of those competitions have restrictions about entering projects that have been entered into other contests.

Second, think about including the photographs when you do press releases.

Third, you might want to use these photos in your advertising, on brochures, or other promotional materials.

Caution: Before you hire any photographer, ask him or her about how he or she handles the copyrights on his or her work. The best circumstance is to arrange for you to own the copyright on the photos so you will not need the photographer's written release for each and every publication of the pictures. If the photographer owns the copyright, he or she has every right to charge you for every time the picture is published—and he or she sets the price.

You may have to pay more to get the copyright, but it can definitely protect you from a lawsuit later. Even if the photographer says he or she gives you the copyright, be sure to get it in writing. If the photographer doesn't have a form, write a short letter for you both to sign stating that the photographer is selling you the copyright to the photos of [item] taken on [date] at [location] and that you are paying him/her $ [make it at least one dollar]. You want to pay the photographer something to show that you have given something of value for the copyright.

Wow! You Won!

Once you are notified that you have won a contest, you need to do some more work to get the most benefit possible from the award.

Talk to the person who is in charge of publicity for the program that is making the award. Ask what he or she plans to do. For example, will he or she:

- Send press releases? If so, where?
- Give the award at a convention?
- Have the award featured in an article in professional magazines?
- Plan other publicity?

You can often help ensure that you get the maximum coverage by suggesting ideas to and helping the publicist. Offer to provide him or her with a list of your local newspapers and magazines (including the names of pertinent editors and their addresses and telephone numbers).

If you know that there will be some fliers, brochures, or magazine articles generated by the awarding organization, ask how many free copies you can have. You also may be able to purchase more copies if you want them. Be sure to ask up front because it is usually less costly to add to a planned print run than to set up and do more later.

Finally, be sure to thank anyone who assisted you in the contest, including:

- Any client who may have been instrumental in helping you win (for instance, the owner of the garden you designed that won the contest).
- Any employees whose work was important to the project.
- The organization that gave the award.
- Anyone else who contributed to your winning (perhaps even past mentors).

SCRATCH EACH OTHER'S BACKS

It may seem a little unusual at first glance, but often you can promote your business by helping other people promote theirs! This has the triple benefit of creating goodwill with your customers, the other business's customers, and the other business owner.

Dave Lakhani of Boise, Idaho offers a perfect example of how that works. Once a year, he puts on a computer swap meet in front of his store, Computer Clearance Center. He sells tables to vendors and individuals to cover his approximately $1,500 in promotional and advertising costs. In addition, he charges large wholesalers 5 percent of their gross at the show.

He regularly draws between three and five thousand people for the event, many of whom have never been to his store before, but many do come back and become regular customers. The event is not only good for the individuals and companies who use this as an opportunity to sell their merchandise, but Lakhani enjoys a hefty average of $15,000 in sales for the day himself.

Another way to work synergistically with other businesses is to talk with your suppliers about co-op promotions they might be interested in funding. In co-op arrangements, the supplier provides funding and/or other assistance to help you with an advertising program or event. There will probably be some requirements that the advertising or event focus primarily on this supplier's products or services, but you may find they are able to assist you with more ideas and support than you ever dreamed.

STUNTS THAT GET YOU NOTICED

Properly done, stunts can attract an incredible amount of attention to your business. Improperly done, they can be a disaster.

Perhaps the classic example of a poorly done stunt was on the television program *WKRP in Cincinnati.* At a Thanksgiving promotion, radio station personnel dropped live turkeys out of a helicopter. Since commercially raised turkeys don't really fly, these birds dropped like stones all over the parking lot, much to the dismay and anguish of the people watching and the radio station staff.

However, there are many, many publicity and/or promotional stunts that occur around you every day that are wildly successful. Some are relatively small, like the local celebrity who raises funds for charity by letting people buy chances to throw pies at his face. Some are much larger, like the artist who paints a mural on a city wall to draw attention to a social problem.

Alan Caruba is a renowned expert at successful stunts although he prefers to call his "events." A consummate public relations professional, Caruba has created fascinating outlets that generate publicity for his business, a positive cash flow in their own right, and an opportunity to educate people while spoofing the media.

Every December, he releases his "Most Boring Celebrities of the Year" list to a few selected media outlets and it gets tremendous exposure. Caruba sees it as a spoof on the serious way much of the media tries to neatly package up the "most" and "best" at the end of every year. In the same vein, he issues press releases of "The Most Boring Films" of the year shortly before the Academy Awards.

Some of his promotions have taken a serious turn that was not originally planned. His Boring Institute was begun as a commentary on the media and how much of popular culture is pretty boring stuff. People who join the Institute can get an authentic Certificate of Membership (for a fee) and order his handheld guide titled *Beating Boredom.* Somewhere along the way, the Institute became what Caruba calls, "the nation's only clearinghouse of information on boredom and the serious personal and social problems it creates such as being a classic sign of depression, suicide, addictions, and crime."

His various media programs have resulted in Caruba becoming a highly sought-after guest for radio and television programs. On the average, he is interviewed over 1,000 times per year as a media critic or because of his Boring Institute and National Anxiety Center, which spoofs media scare campaigns. These appearances also serve to promote his public relations business and get information about his publications out to the public.

Caruba counsels people considering this type of event promotion to realize that the keys to making it work are excellent research and targeted media placements. For example, he keeps a file all year of movie reviews to help him determine the "Most Boring Films." Targeting the media placements means that he sends his press releases to the wire services and other recipients who are most likely to give them wide exposure.

Coming Up with Perfect Promotions

How do you come up with promotions? One way is to pay attention to promotional activities other businesses are doing. You won't want to copy them very closely because then there won't be a clear connection in the potential customer's mind between the promotion and your business.

A good place to look for ideas is in the magazines that serve other businesses similar to yours. For instance, if you are in the teleservice industry, you probably read magazines like *Teleprofessional* and *Telemarketing.* If you are in the beverage/bottling industry, you might read *Beverage World* or *Southern Beverage Journal.* You probably already receive a number of publications targeted toward your particular kind of business. In most cases, these magazines publish either feature stories or short, press-release-style pieces about how others have successfully used promotional activities to boost their businesses.

Also, keep an eye out for interesting promotions when you travel and even when you read general business publications or publications targeting other businesses. You may stumble on an exciting idea that was successful for someone else even though it may need a little reworking to intrigue your target audience.

As you plan your promotional events, keep the fun factor mentioned at the beginning of the chapter in mind. People are much more likely to come to your event if they think it will be fun for them than if they think it will be good for them. Whenever you can, it is a good idea to incorporate extra fun elements into your event such as:

- Food. If it is not in your budget, perhaps you can make arrangements with another business owner who has a restaurant or even a hot dog or popcorn cart.
- Music. There is nothing like music to help set the tone. Hire up-beat country western fiddlers for a cowboy-themed event or a string quartet for an upscale, classical event. If you want to play pre-recorded music, please see page 134.
- Entertainment. The entertainment should match the tone of the event. If you have a circus theme, hire clowns. If you have access to a well-known celebrity, ask them to make an appearance and possibly sign autographs. Check with your suppliers to see if they have access to any well-known people as a result of their sponsorships. For example, Olympic athletes often visit businesses that have supported their athletic dreams.

AWARD PROGRAMS THAT PUT YOU IN THE SPOTLIGHT

Giving awards might seem like a strange way to promote your business, but it can have marvelous results in terms of getting free publicity and making your business better known and respected by the very people you want as customers.

Perhaps the most important factor to consider in creating an award program is determining exactly what you hope to achieve through it. Do you want to get better known locally? Do you want to be noticed by a specific group of people? Are you hoping to achieve regional and/or national recognition or even notoriety?

There will be some costs associated with giving awards, but they can be kept to a minimum. The costs will fall generally into two categories:(1) the award itself and (2) publicizing the award.

The award should tie into the kind of business you operate. For example, if you have a bookstore that focuses on children's books, you might work with the local elementary schools. Target one or two grade levels to work with. Then arrange to award any child in those grades who reads a certain number of books (a determination you reach with the teachers) an award certificate and a coupon that gives a dollar figure ($1 or $5) off a future purchase. The coupon will bring the winners into your store where they are likely to make purchases in excess of the value of the award coupon.

The certificates can be very inexpensive. Most stationery stores sell packages of printed certificates that can be customized. Some papers even have beautiful backgrounds and borders in which you can print whatever you like on them. Most computers will allow you to create a layout for your certificate using different fonts and letter sizes. Leave a blank space on the certificate so you can type in the name of the award winner to make it more personal. Be sure to have the name of your business prominently included on the certificate and consider having a line or two on the bottom where you and perhaps the school principal can sign the certificates. If you want to get very fancy, attach a gold or silver adhesive seal to the certificate (seals are also available at stationery stores).

To get the maximum advantage from such a program, try to arrange with the school to present the certificates at an awards assembly in school or at a parents' club function. This gets your business name in front of more people and reminds them not only about the products you offer, but that you support the education of young people.

When you are planning the award ceremony, write a press release (see Chapter 4) for your local newspapers mentioning the award and the names of the children who won it. You can even have a picture taken of a child receiving the award and submit it with the press release. Many papers are looking for good news, especially about young people, and may give your press release good coverage.

What other kinds of awards are likely to increase public awareness about your business without having to deal with contests? Suppose you have a sporting goods store called Winning Sports. Talk with a sportswriter at the local newspaper or radio station about creating a "Winning Sports' Athlete of the Week" award. The sportswriter picks a local athlete to recognize once a week and does a short write-up. From the writer's point of view, it gets people looking for his byline; your benefit is that your store's name is mentioned prominently in the name of the award every week. Again, you will probably want to provide a certificate of recognition and possibly a coupon or discount certificate to bring the winner into your store.

DON'T FORGET THE FUN

As you have seen, there is an incredible variety of ways you can promote your business for free or at a low cost. All of them will require some commitment of time and energy from you and properly done, they hold the promise of new customers/clients and more business. Pick the one(s) that sound like fun to you. After all, when you are enjoying yourself, your attitude will be transmitted to the others involved and they will catch your energy and enthusiasm.

SELF-SURVEY: WORKSHEET FOR PLANNING EVENTS THAT ARE FUN AND EFFECTIVE

The goal I hope to achieve through this event: _____

_____

Type of event planned: _____

_____

Pre-event publicity (for example, press releases, radio announcements, and mailings to customers): _____

_____

_____

_____

Planning schedule:

    1 month before: _____

    2 weeks before: _____

    1 week before: _____

    Day before: _____

    Day of event: _____

Supplies needed: _____

Employees/Others needed to help: _____

_____

_____

Post-event publicity planned: _____

_____

4

Getting the Media to Notice You

The artist Andy Warhol is credited with saying, "In the future, everyone will be world-famous for fifteen minutes," and you have undoubtedly heard people remark that this person or that person has just had "their 15 minutes."

It is absolutely true that the media can make you famous almost instantly. The trick is to be noticed for the reasons you want to be noticed—and at the time you choose. By carefully crafting your approach to the media, you can create the image and transmit the message that will be the most beneficial to your business. Working with the media also has the advantage of getting you great coverage for a minimal investment in your time and money.

You also will find that as you develop media contacts, others will search you out. In fact, once you are recognized as an expert by one media outlet, others will often begin seeking your opinion/expertise when they need similar information. It helps if you are the local expert on a subject. But even if there are others who are as knowledgeable as you (or possibly even more so), you will find that good press releases can get you the media recognition as the expert in the public's mind.

The benefits of being recognized as the media's expert will vary depending on your kind of business. However, you can expect that the benefits you achieve will include enhanced professional standing (both with the public and your peers) and inquiries from the people who hear or read about you and who want to become customers or clients.

STEP-BY-STEP TO DYNAMIC PRESS RELEASES

A press release is a wonderful tool you can use to get the media to notice you. It is relatively simple and inexpensive to create yourself and can open doors for you at newspapers, magazines, radio stations, and even television stations.

You will find that there are two major times you will want to use a press release. The first is when you are announcing an upcoming event. The purpose of this release is to get the editor or producer interested in covering your event and/or getting them to notify the public about this upcoming event. The subject of your release must be newsworthy. For example, no editor is likely to care about your semi-annual sale (that would be an advertising subject). However, the editor might be interested to find that you are sponsoring a softball tournament to benefit a local children's charity. Other excellent times for such press releases can be when:

- You or your business receive an award.
- You become an officer in a professional organization.
- A new development or discovery occurs in your industry.
- You are anticipating seasonally oriented story needs by the media (for example, when editors are preparing "back to school" stories, they may value information on everything from how to pack a healthy lunch to which immunizations a child needs).

The second time you need to send a press release is when there is a news event going on and you are capable of giving information that would help the media prepare their stories.

It is extremely important to consider the time factor for these releases. You must be able to sit down and write them immediately and fax them or have them delivered within hours, before the media find a different authority to interview or quote. An example of when this kind of press release might be used is after a natural disaster. An insurance agent could help the media alert people on how to file insurance claims. Another situation could be an attorney who might be qualified to comment on the legal aspects of a notorious and ongoing lawsuit to help people understand it and how the situations that develop in that suit compare to local laws and practice. Other excellent examples of when this type of press release might be used include:

- Giving the media an expert (you) to refute negative impressions they are distributing that come from others
- Alerting the media to breaking news in your business or industry that will affect the public
- Giving information about a survey you did that involves your business and the people in the community
- Ensuring the media designate you as their expert commentator/interviewee on any story that could affect your business.

There are three keys to writing a successful press release that you must always keep in mind.

 Timeliness. Your press release must impart a sense of urgency. If you are notifying the media about an upcoming event, call the appropriate departments ahead of time to find out how long before the event they need to have the press release and who exactly you should direct it to. When you are writing about a news event that you or your business have an interest in, you will need to get it to the appropriate editor or producer immediately (within hours).

Brevity. Remember, you aren't writing the whole story in a press release. It's purpose is to inspire the editor or producer to do a story on your topic. A good press release should never be more than two pages—and one page is preferred.

 Excitement. Your press release must give the reader a sense that this is an important story that he or she needs to cover right now. You have to make it stand out from all the other press releases that person has received today and make it irresistible to that person who is assigning stories to reporters.

There is a basic format that your press release should follow (see example that follows). It is simple and straightforward. You can make some minor changes, but be sure that your release includes all the elements in this format example. Two completed press releases are included as examples later in this chapter. The numbers refer to an explanation of that element that is explained in the section following the example.

```
                    Letterhead (1)

To: (e.g., business editor) (2) FOR IMMEDIATE RELEASE (4)
Contact: Name (3)          Date: 0/00/00 (5)

             REALLY HOT TITLE (6)

Attention grabbing first paragraph (7)

Important facts paragraph (that is, who, what,
when, where) (8)

Why you? Why now? (9)

[The body of the press release should be double
spaced. If you must use more than one page, put "-
more-" at the bottom of the first page and "###" or
"-30-" at the end of the release.]

Include a photograph if applicable (10)
```

Writing a Press Release by the Numbers

Following is an explanation of the numbered items in the sample press release.

1. Use your letterhead when you send the press release. It helps establish a professional image for you and your expertise.

2. Whenever possible, address your release to a real person and be sure it is the right person. If you don't know who the right person is, call the station or newspaper and ask the receptionist. Be sure you get the correct spelling of the name and you know the gender (there are plenty of people with names such as Kim, Leslie, and Pat who could be either men or women). If you are sending this release to several offices, print out a fresh one for each office and address each release to the correct person.

3. The contact name here refers to the person that the media should contact if they want more information on the subject of your release. It can be you, your secretary, or another employee. That person should know he or she is listed so there are no awkward situations when the media call. If he or she is not especially knowledgeable about your information, it is absolutely appropriate that they act as an intermediary and put the caller through to you. If your letterhead does not have your address and telephone and fax numbers, put them under the contact name so the editor or producer can find you easily.

4. The statement, "FOR IMMEDIATE RELEASE" tells the editor or producer that he or she may use this information right now. If you want either of them to know about something early enough to research a story on it, but don't want it publicized yet, replace the phrase with, "EMBARGOED UNTIL DATE." The date you give should be the first day you are willing to have this story available to the public.

5. The date you put here is the date you send the release. The purpose of this is to help the editor or producer know how timely this information is.

6. The importance of an exciting title cannot be overstated. It should be truthful and something you can support in the body of your release. A title such as "Interstellar Aliens Shop at Local Market" will get you noticed—and laughed at—but it is not likely to generate any coverage and will make you appear unprofessional. A better title would be, "Local Therapist Aids Children Traumatized by Shooter." The first thing that will be read on your release is the title. If your title does not give a sense that it contains a story, the rest of your release will probably never be read.

7. If the editor or producer gets past the title, the place where you sell them or lose them is in your first paragraph. It is critically important that you do a great selling job here on the story you want them to cover. Make it exciting. Give it a sense of urgency.

8. In this paragraph, include any other important facts that will be needed by the editor or producer to determine if they want to cover the story. It can also include brief quotes from one or two people who are important to the event.

9. If you have not already explained why you are the expert or why you are submitting this release, do so in this paragraph. The information should be brief; the editor or producer doesn't need your entire resume, they just want to know why you consider yourself the expert. If this is a release announcing an award, promotion, etc., you can give a little extra background information in this paragraph. Also, if you have not already mentioned it, this is the place where you explain the timeliness of your story.

10. It is always a good idea to include a photograph if you can. If you are sending it to print media, look at a sample to see if they normally use color or black and white photos and send what they use. A head shot is always a good idea, but if your release is about an event, a good photograph of the preparations or the actual event can help sell the story. If the release is going to a television station, a photograph can help the producer see how you might look on his or her program and make the producer more comfortable about contacting you.

Here are two different kinds of press releases you may want to send. The facts are imaginary, but the concept is real. The first one is sent to the business editor of the local newspaper to announce a new business associate or employee. Most newspapers will do listings of this sort of information at least once a week. If possible, include a head shot photograph.

```
The Homey-House Real Estate Company
123 Cozy Lane
Hometown, USA

To: Ima Writer, Business Editor FOR IMMEDIATE RELEASE
    BreakingNews Times

Contact: Shirley Helpful  Date: January 1, 2000
         (800) 555-1212

    AWARD-WINNING AGENT JOINS HOMEY-HOUSE TEAM
```

Ura Client, president of Homey-House Real Estate Brokerage in Hometown, is pleased to announce that award-winning real estate agent Primo Sellers has joined the firm.

Client says, "Sellers is a proven professional with over twenty years' experience in helping home buyers and sellers in the Hometown area. We are delighted that he has chosen to join our organization."

Sellers has been the top selling agent in the county for the last two years and has won the prestigious Golden Key award from the local Association of Realtors. He can be reached by calling (800) 555-1212, extension 777. A photo is attached.

# # #

The second imaginary press release is going to the same editor and it is designed to attract media attention to an event you are holding. Only send a photograph if it relates to the event. The idea with this kind of release is to convince the press that this is news they want to cover.

ACME Hardware Store
456 Hammer Drive
Tooltown, USA

To: Ima Writer, Business Editor FOR IMMEDIATE RELEASE
    BreakingNews Times

Contact: Rocky Rhoades   Date: January 1, 2000
         (800) 555-1212

TV STAR TO "PAINT TOOLTOWN"

I.M. "Splatter" King, the star of TV's "Fix This
House" program and national spokesperson for
Sticks-Well Paints, will be at ACME Hardware on
January 31 to demonstrate correct painting
techniques in his world "Paint Your Town" tour.

Splat, as he is know to his television fans, will
appear at the store from noon until 3 pm to do a
live demonstration and answer questions from the
public. Some of the techniques he will demonstrate
are brush painting, roller painting, trim work, and
sponge painting. Selected attendees will be given
an opportunity to work with Splat.

Also during the demonstration, there will be a
drawing for a chance to have a walk-on part on an
episode of "Fix This House."

ACME Hardware manager Rocky Rhoades says, "We are
honored to have this opportunity to bring such a
well-respected paint expert and much-beloved
television personality to Hometown. We are looking
forward to this opportunity to help local residents
with their painting questions."

After the demonstration, Splat will sign autographs
and refreshments will be available.

For more information, please call Rocky Rhoades at
the number above. To reach Splat's agent, call
(800) 555-1234.

# # #

GETTING THE EDITOR OF YOUR NEWSPAPER TO NOTICE YOU

If you pick up your local newspaper and thumb through it, looking at the sheer volume of material that the editors must generate every day, you will understand why editors are almost always looking for a good story or a local expert they can quote for their stories.

Your press release can be an excellent way to get an editor interested in you and your business. However, there is nothing like developing a relationship with an editor to enhance the possibility that your releases will get a positive reading.

There are several accepted ways you can approach an editor. One way to start is by keeping an eye out for community meetings where editors may be speaking or socializing. It is appropriate to introduce yourself and briefly explain who you are and what you do. It can be helpful to add that you have a story idea you would like to share with them and ask if they would prefer a press release or to have you make an appointment to come in and talk it over with them.

Don't try to monopolize their time at these events because you will only end up irritating them. After talking to editors, either call for appointments or send the press releases within the time you specified (usually a week).

If you are comfortable using a personal approach, call an editor and ask for an appointment even if you have never met. Be flexible and willing to meet at the editor's convenience because his or her schedule is likely to be extremely tight. Be prepared to be warm and cordial and make your point briefly and succinctly.

It is a good idea to have a press release, and possibly even a resume outlining your expertise, to leave with the editor. Dress professionally so you can make a good impression. However, don't be disappointed if your initial contact does not result in a story. Ask the editor what kinds of stories he or she is looking for, and you can keep an eye out to developing press releases in the future that will interest him or her.

Once you have sent a press release to an editor, do not pester him or her about when he or she is going to run an article on your story. Editors tend to take a dim view of people who start calling daily as soon as they mail the press release and keep calling in hopes that the editors will assign the story just to get rid of them.

The proper etiquette is to wait until the editor has had your release for about five days. If you have not heard anything, call and ask if the editor received it and if they have any questions. If the editor says that he or she is not interested in your story, ask what kinds of stories they are especially looking for. If you get the editor's voice mail and they do not return your call, you can usually assume that the editor is not interested at this time. Continue to read the publication and try again later with another press release that you think will interest the editor.

FREE WAYS TO GET ON THE RADIO

Radio is a marvelous medium for getting free publicity for you and your business. When you send your press release to radio producers, consider sending a brief audio tape of you either on another show or speaking in front of a group. The producer will probably only listen to a minute or two, but it will demonstrate that you can speak clearly and coherently.

There are several ways you can approach the concept of being on the radio. For instance, would you prefer to be:

- *The commentator.* If you are wearing this hat, you are the expert that the news department calls when it is working on stories that cover your area of expertise. The commentator should expect to be called on short notice to do brief interviews when stories related to their specialty are in the news.

- *The personality.* When you aim for this position, you could be anything from the person a radio talk show uses regularly to expound a point of view to an expert who has a regularly scheduled show or segment that relates to your business. This could cover everything from an investment professional who comments on the daily changes in the stock market to a pediatrician on a call-in show who helps parents of young children. This type of commitment is usually easier to schedule and in some instances, your participation may be able to be recorded in advance.

- *The guest.* Many programs have interviews with invited experts that can last anywhere from five minutes to an hour. You are normally booked for these spots in advance and the bookings may be generated by your press release. If you write a book about your specialty, you will be especially interesting to the producers of these programs.

One advantage of being on radio is that it is an especially cost effective way to promote yourself. In most cases, your costs will only be the expense of creating and sending the press release. If a radio station wants to do a phone interview, which is quite common, the producer will arrange to call you so the station pays for the toll charges.

Whenever you are notified that a radio station wants to interview you, it is a good idea to arrange to do it from a telephone located in a quiet place and free of background noise that could make it difficult for listeners to hear you. Before you go on the air, be sure you know the name of the host, where the station is (especially if you are promoting yourself around the country), and the correct call letters. It is considered good etiquette to mention the host and station during the interview and let the host say nice things about your expertise and/or products. If you spend a lot of time talking about yourself and your products, you could sound self-centered and boorish.

Another tip is to *not* have your call waiting activated on the phone line during the interview. Radio hosts often try to make it sound like you are there in the studio with them. Having your call waiting interrupt the interview destroys that illusion.

Utilizing the Public Service Announcement

There can be times when getting the radio station to air Public Service Announcements (PSAs) can be a valuable promotional tool for you and your business.

Stations are most likely to welcome your PSAs when you are having an event or promotion that involves your joint efforts with community organizations or charities (as discussed in Chapters 1 through 3). The key is to keep the announcements short (ten to thirty seconds) and write them in a language style similar to the style the on-air personalities use. If you listen carefully, you will notice a difference in the ways that a rock station and a country/western station announce the same event.

The format for creating your PSA should be similar to the following sample:

```
                     Letterhead
To: (for example, show producer)

FOR IMMEDIATE RELEASE

Contact: Name Date: 0/00/00

:15 (for a 15 second announcement)

Announcer: (Body of the PSA)
```

Once you have written the PSA, read it aloud several times and time yourself using the second-hand on a clock. Be careful not to try to make it too detailed, or the announcer will not be able to read it in the time allotted. Include a phone number where listeners can call for more information. Also, if you use any words or names that might be difficult to pronounce, give a phonetic (fo net'ik) pronunciation for them.

SECRETS THAT MAKE TV PRODUCERS CALL YOU

Do you ever wonder how so many people get on television? Would you like to be one of them? The key to attracting the attention of television producers is to have an interesting angle and a strong visual component to your press release or proposal.

When you send your press release to a television program producer, it is an excellent idea to send a photograph of yourself (maybe doing your skill) or even a brief (five-minute) videotape of you doing a different television program. The producer will not be bothered if it is a program on a competing station. He or she is just trying to see how you look and behave in front of a camera. If you have never appeared on television, have a friend tape you in front of a group where you are speaking, or you can even set up the opportunity and have family and friends be your audience.

Some opportunities to propose appearances are obvious. If you have a garden store, you can write a press release extolling your ability to show viewers everything from how to prune roses in the winter to how to identify and fight garden pests in the summer. (Of course, you should only propose one topic per press release.) If you are a caterer or have a kitchen supply store, consider proposing a segment showing viewers how to make quick holiday candy or nutritious after school snacks.

If you do a good job with your segment, the producer will be open to future proposals from you and you could even develop a schedule of regular appearances. What would you like to do on television? You might have to watch some programs for a while before you determine which ones are most likely to be a good match for your specialty.

Start by approaching local television programs. They are the most likely to welcome you. They also can be a great training ground where you can develop your on-camera skills. As you develop these skills, you can approach the larger, national programs. After all, they already have other professionals on from time to time, why shouldn't you be one?

Look Like a Professional

People often worry about the wrong thing when they are getting ready to make a television appearance. A common worry is "What if the camera adds 10 pounds?" Actually, unless you are there to promote a weight loss program, that should be the least of your concerns. As an expert, you want to look like someone that the viewers will want to search out. To help you achieve that look, take some dressing tips from newscasters and talk show hosts.

- Keep your clothing comfortable so that viewers pay attention to your message, not to how often you pulled and tugged at your clothes.

- Wear solid colors. Have you ever sat and watched someone on television who was wearing a plaid or patterned outfit and the pattern seemed to jump off the outfit or change colors right in front of your eyes? Do you remember what that person was talking about? Thought not. It is best to wear solid, muted, or dark colors. White and bright red can do some fascinating things in front of a camera. That doesn't rule out a white shirt or blouse under a jacket, it is just that large expanses of these colors tend to take on a life of their own.

- Be sure of your hair and makeup. Your hair should not cover most of your face so that you look like a talking mop. Cameras like to see your eyes and so do viewers. Women, your makeup should probably be a little more pronounced than what you wear on the street, but don't put on so much that it distracts from your message. Men should not be uncomfortable with a little makeup to smooth out facial coloring or a dusting of powder to take the shine off a nervous brow. Do not expect the television program to do your hair and/or makeup unless the producer offered that when the segment was booked.

What to Take to Your TV Appearance

When you are going to do a television appearance, there are several things you should take with you.

Always have some business cards. Be sure to leave one at the switchboard in case there are callers after the appearance who want to get in touch with you.

If you are there to promote a book or product, be sure you have at least one with you. Even if samples were sent ahead, they may have gotten lost or misappropriated. It is also a nice touch to give books or samples to the switchboard operator, producer you worked with, and even the interviewer if they don't already have them.

Once You Get Your Media Exposure

Once you have achieved the media exposure you have sought by sending your press releases, there is one more short writing assignment you need to complete—a thank you note.

Editors and producers create wonderful opportunities for people to promote their businesses, but they rarely receive the thanks they deserve from the people who benefit most. If you visit their offices, you will often see a few yellowing thank you notes tacked up on their bulletin boards. You can also bet that when they need an expert in the future, they will remember the people who took a moment to say thank you.

A good thank you note does not have to be a literary masterpiece. All you need to do is write a few lines thanking them for the opportunity and perhaps mentioning something about the article or segment that especially pleased you or a good result that was achieved because of their efforts.

SELF-SURVEY: WORKSHEET FOR DEVELOPING AN ACTION PLAN FOR MEDIA EXPOSURE

Goal of media exposure: _____

Newspaper(s): _____

Editor/Department: _____

Address: _____

_____

Telephone number: _____

Topic of press release: _____

Date sent: _____

Date followed up: _____

Result: _____

_____

Radio station(s)

Call letters: _____

Name of program targeted: _____

Name of program host: _____

Name of program producer: _____

Address: _____

_____

Telephone number: _____

Topic of press release: _____

Date sent: _____

Date followed up: _____

Result: _____

_____

Television station(s)

Station name: _____

Network affiliation: _____

Name of program targeted: _____

Name of program host: _____

Name of program producer: _____

Address: _____

_____

Telephone number: _____

Topic of press release: _____

Date sent: _____

Date followed up: _____

Result: _____

_____

5

Getting Published = Getting Known

Have you ever thought that the people who write articles and books know some special secrets that you'll never fathom? Do they seem somehow more authoritative? More interesting? Would you like to be one of them?

Perhaps you've wondered if having books and articles published could help you promote your business. Yes, it can! The benefits are tremendous and long-lasting. Think of all the times you've kept an article or book because you believed you might need that information again some day. Everyone does it.

Every one of those publications was written by someone. Someone who wanted to get a reputation as an expert in his or her field. Someone who wanted others to seek them out when they needed goods or services like the ones he or she offers. Or maybe it was someone who just wanted to share information that could help other people.

DON'T FALL FOR THESE MYTHS

Surprisingly, many people start out facing one of two writing myths that, if believed, can keep them from successfully getting published.

The first myth might be something you would never expect, that writing is easy—after all, you've been doing it since the first grade. The problem with this myth is that like anything else in life, when you are overconfident, you tend to get lazy and not do your best work.

The second myth is that writing books and articles is too difficult. When people believe this, often they are remembering their school days when teachers gave them topics to write on and then apparently gleefully, proceeded to cover those carefully wrought pages with red or blue scribbles highlighting failures in logic, syntax, and spelling.

Not surprisingly, people often got the message that they were incapable of good writing. Fortunately, that is not usually true. When you sit down to write, you will remember many of the lessons those teachers were trying to impress on you. You'll probably discover that you are a better writer than you thought—in part because of those lessons.

Writing Techniques

There are some key techniques that professional writers often use that you can utilize to help ensure that your message gets across in your writing. These are the general things you need to be thinking about on any writing project. Later in the chapter, the techniques will be handled in more detail specifically for article and book projects.

 Create an outline. Don't worry about having it fit some special pattern you learned in school. The purpose of this outline is to help you think through the piece you want to write. In fact, it may look more like a list than an outline. The important thing is to create the framework for your article or book. Quite often, the outline for a book will look like a table of contents. Just as the planning phase of any project takes a bit of time, don't rush this phase. Consider these questions as you write your outline:

- What message do you want to give to your readers?

- What information do you want to include? (Often, the best way to think of this is "What questions would I ask if I didn't know anything about this subject?")
- What order should it be in? (It is especially important to have a strong opening and ending.)

Choose excellent experts. In nearly every persuasive book or article, the writer is authoritative, but still uses quotes from or references to other experts or resources. Sometimes inexperienced writers are afraid that quoting other experts will somehow dilute their personal impact. Actually, just the opposite occurs. When it is apparent to readers that you not only write with authority, but can include other reference material and quotes, it shows your superior grasp of the subject.

Deal with deadlines. Too often, people have a student mentality that they will write their project the night before it is due. Don't do it. Plan ahead. The professional way to handle any writing project is to get started early (if for no other reason than that this allows you time to find that last anecdote or fact you discover you need). Also allow yourself time to put the article aside to "rest" for a day or more after you finish it.

Edit yourself. Once your project has rested for a day or more, go back and read it again. Sometimes things that made perfect sense when you write them can be unclear the next day. One technique that can help tremendously is to read the piece out loud to yourself. This will help you catch run-on sentences and places that may read a little awkwardly.

This is also a time to check to be sure you have not changed voices or tenses in the piece. Fix any inconsistencies. You may think that handling these details is the editor's job, and in a sense it is. However, if you turn in a manuscript that is sloppily written, you not only reduce your chances of getting it published, you risk being branded as a person who does not do quality work—and that's certainly not the image you are striving for through your writing.

Consider peer review. This can work one of two ways. First, have a trusted colleague read the piece. Get their honest opinion about it. Ask what they thought it was about and what they learned from it. Then ask yourself, is that what I meant to say? If not, you need to revise your work.

Second, have a trusted friend who doesn't necessarily know anything about your business read the article. Get his or her honest opinion and ask them the same questions you asked your colleague. Again, ask yourself if that was what you were trying to convey. Ask your friend if they have any questions about your topic. This answer can show you where you might need to add information that will be important and valuable to your readers.

 Create an attractive product. Just as you work hard to present your products and services in the best possible light to potential customers, you need to present your article or book to the publisher in the most professional manner. Your work should be printed on one side of white pages. It should be double-spaced. There should be adequate margins for the editor to make comments in. You should also be able to send a copy of the book or article on a disk in a computer language that the editor can access on her computer. Call the editor and ask which program he or she uses. If you cannot translate your material to that format, many copy shops or small word processing businesses can do it for you for a nominal cost.

ARTICLE BASICS

There are some basic techniques you can use to make the best use of your time and talents when you are writing an article.

1. Determine your goal. Before you begin an article project, ask yourself what you hope to achieve through this piece. Do you want increased awareness of your products/services

with potential customers? Are you working to increase your recognition in your industry? Are you trying to position yourself as an expert on the subject so you will be sought out by television and radio programs? After you determine your goal, decide what you need to do or say in the article to achieve your goal.

2. Decide who is your target audience. By now, you know who your customers are. Think of them in terms of demographics. What is their age group? What is their income? Where do they live? Where do they work? If your target is your professional peer group, what publications do they respect? If your target is more media attention, where would the media look to find an expert like you?

3. Consider your market. Which publications would help you best reach your target audience? Check the masthead (the list of editors—usually toward the front of the magazine) and compare it to the authors of the articles. If the articles are not all staff-written, good! The editors may be looking for well-written articles. Even if the magazine articles are mostly staff-written, it can't hurt to propose an article; they may just be interested.

   Do not think that you have to start at the top with the most prestigious publications. Many local newspapers and small regional publications, even those shoppers that come in the mail or are in a rack at the grocery store, are excellent places to consider as markets for your articles. For instance, if you sell landscaping supplies, you might do a monthly article about seasonal flowers or planting preparations. Sometimes these smaller publications will also give you a byline and a note at the bottom of the article telling readers how to find you or they may even be willing to give you advertising space in exchange for your article.

4. Analyze the publication. How long are the articles that are similar to the one you want to write? If the publication has covered a similar subject recently, how will yours be different? Does it use a lot of quotes from outside experts? Statistics? Examples? Can you supply the same types of sources in your piece?

5. Focus, focus, focus. Be sure that what you want to write about is something you can handle in the length you plan to write. For instance, an article on handling business finances is a good idea, but it could more easily be a book than an article. Learning to handle the cash flow statement is more tightly focused and therefore more likely to work as an article.

6. Plan. OK, this is the time you need to revert to those early writing lessons in school. Some people find that starting by creating an outline helps them organize their thoughts. Think about the anecdotes, resources, and quotes you want to use. Do you have them? If they are from people's personal experience or copyrighted material, do you have written permission to use them from either the person who experienced the event or the writer or organization that holds the copyright?

7. Write a proposal letter. Get the name of the articles editor or editor-in-chief from the magazine's masthead. Look there for the address of the magazine and often the telephone number—be sure you get the address for the editorial department and not the advertising or subscription addresses.

   Write an exciting one- or two-page letter offering to write your article for the magazine. Start with a "hook" sentence to get the editor excited about your idea. Then explain a little about what you plan to cover, experts you plan to use, and why you are the person to write this article.

   Remember, this proposal is a sales document, so be willing to spend some time on it getting it just right. You should hear from the editor after two to six weeks. If you are turned down, analyze your proposal to see if you can strengthen it, then submit it to another publication. If the editor gets in touch and wants your article, you are ready to:

8. Write it. Don't worry about making the first draft perfect. Get your thoughts down. Use the outline to help you. Let your energy and enthusiasm for your topic shine through. If you want resources to help you with the writing to be sure you use correct style and have variety in your use of language, you can consult *The Associated Press Stylebook, The Chicago Manual of Style,* and *Roget's International Thesaurus* (see Resources).

9. Cool it! Once you have written something, let it cool down for a day or two and then read it to see if it really says what you want it to say. Sometimes it helps to read it out loud to catch the flow (especially if you tend to write run-on sentences).

10. Think peer review. If you are a novice at writing for publication, have a trusted peer or friend read the piece. Ask if it made sense. Then ask the most important question: What did you learn from it? If your peer or friend says they got your message, congratulations! You were successful. If he or she says something completely different, perhaps you need to rewrite the article. Or maybe you'll discover that they got even more from your writing than you expected.

11. Submit it. The editor will tell you (or you should ask) how he or she wants your article sent in. Many publishers now want it on disk, but others still want a "hard copy," which is the article printed on paper. It should be printed double-spaced on white paper with your name on the first page. Please never send handwritten copy to an editor. It makes you look like an amateur and can give the editor a negative impression of your competence.

12. Enjoy the results! You may be pleasantly surprised at how many people will mention that they saw your article and how long the kudos keep coming in. Now, what will your next article be about?

PUBLISHING A BOOK CAN HELP YOUR BUSINESS GROW

Being the author of a book published about some facet of your business or industry gives you tremendous stature in our society. Just walk around any bookstore and you will see that there are currently books available on any topic you can think of. If all those people could write books, you can, too.

Book Basics

There are some basic steps you need to follow to write a book like a professional writer. The process is simple, but you will need to invest a substantial amount of time. Here is what you need to know to write a book.

1. First determine your goal. What do you hope to achieve through this project? Then before you begin, decide what you need to do or say in the book to achieve that goal.

2. Decide who is your target audience. By now, you know who your customers are. Now think of them in terms of demographics. What is their age group? What is their income? Where do they live? Where do they work?

3. Consider your market. This will take a little research. Start by looking in *Books in Print* at your local library. Check to see if there are any other books like the one you want to write.

   Go to a library and/or bookstore. Look at the books that are on similar topics. How is your idea different? Make a list of the competition and write a sentence or paragraph explaining how your book will be different and better. You will need this when you are writing your book proposal.

   Which of the books would be complementary to yours? Call their publishers and ask for a copy of their catalogs to be sure. When you write your book proposal, showing how your book can fill a gap in their catalogs can be an excellent selling point to publishers.

4. Focus. Once you know what your competition is, you can develop a focus for your book that makes it stand apart from the rest. For example, if you are in the real estate industry, you certainly might want to write about real estate. However, when you study the competition, you realize that the books being published are targeting one segment of the real estate market such as buying, selling, or investing. In fact, the best kind of focus often takes it down another level so that rather than writing a book about buying real estate, you might want to consider focusing your book by demographics (such as buying a home when you're single), or geographic area (buying a home in California), or some other niche that your research shows is underserved but large enough to interest a publisher.

5. Plan your book. Start by developing a table of contents. This will help you organize your thoughts. Then for each heading in the table of contents, write a short description of what you plan to put in this section (or chapter). You may find as you do this step that your original plan included too much information in some sections and not enough in others. If so, reorganize the material until the sections will be approximately the same length.

As you plan the book, start thinking about where you will find any information you need and do not currently have. One easy system is to have a file folder for each section or chapter. As you do the research and accumulate information and data, slip the materials you acquire into the folder for that section. This will save you endless hours of looking for information that can get lost when research material is just kept in boxes or stacks.

Note: If you find copyrighted materials, whether they are text, charts, or graphics, that you think you would like to use, now is a good time to write to the copyright holder and ask permission to use the material. You don't want to wait until the last minute because reputable publishers often ask for written proof of permission to use copyrighted materials before they accept your manuscript.

6. Write your book proposal. Because a book is a much larger project than an article, a book proposal is more detailed than an article proposal letter. There are six basic areas you will want to cover in your proposal.

   A. Sell the idea. Use your best writing skills to convince the editor that you have a great idea for a book and are the best person to write it.

   B. Show the publisher the market. Demonstrate why there is a market for your book and who will buy it by using examples and possibly even statistics. This is a good place to mention anything you plan to do to help promote the book (for example, write articles, do interviews, or give seminars).

   C. List your competition. It sounds irrational because you would assume that most acquisition editors already know the competition. This is a place to show that you've done your homework and you know how your book will rise above the competition.

D. Provide a table of contents. Include the explanations for the different chapters/sections to show the editor you have thought the project through.

E. Write one or more chapters. They do not have to be the first chapters, but they should be typical of the material in the book so that the editor can evaluate your writing style and your grasp of the material.

F. Extra materials. This is where you include your resume or curriculum vitae and any supporting materials that might interest the editor such as articles you have published on this topic. If you have said you can give interviews to promote the book, include a head shot photograph of yourself and possibly even an audiotape if you often speak on this topic. These can help the editor sell your book to the publisher based on your ability to help promote it.

Whew! That looks like a lot of work—and it is, if you do it right. Just as you work hard to create the right image and reputation for your business, you need to create a book proposal that puts your best foot forward. Remember, it is a sales document for a specialized audience, so it needs to include all the information that audience expects.

The proposal should be typed, double-spaced, on white paper. Your name and contact information should be on the first page and your name and the name of your book should be on the top of every other page.

Never just send your proposal addressed to "editor." In all likelihood, it will end up in a slush pile and may be read months later—and then by a "reader," not an editor.

When you have identified the publisher you want to work with, call the company before you send your proposal. Ask the receptionist two important questions:

- Does your publishing house read unagented proposals? (If not, you probably need an agent, and the best ones are difficult to get if you don't already have a track record as a writer or are not a celebrity).

■ What is the name of the editor who handles manuscripts similar to mine? Be sure to get the spelling right and if the name is the least bit ambiguous, ask for the editor's gender (after all, Lee, Pat, or Kim could be either men or women).

If you are lucky enough to know someone who has recently had a book published on a topic similar to yours, if their book is complementary rather than competitive with yours, and if you are considering approaching the same publisher, ask your friend for the name of her editor and if you can use your friend's name when contacting that editor. This tactic can often get prompt attention for your proposal.

7. Sign a contract. When a publisher agrees to publish your book, you will be offered a written contract. Read it carefully. You might even want to hire an attorney who specializes in intellectual property law to review it with you to be sure you understand it completely. If there are some clauses that make you uncomfortable, you may be able to negotiate some changes. Just be aware that few publishers give large advances on first books, so don't plan any major extravagances until your royalty checks come in.

8. Start writing your book. Even while you are waiting for a decision from the editor, you can continue to collect information and begin writing. It is best to get busy writing while you are excited about the project. If you put it aside while the proposal is being considered, you may find it difficult to get back into the swing of the project. Also, if an editor wants the book done quickly, you'll have a head start.

9. Watch for continuity. Writing a book takes a long time and involves a lot of work. From time to time, review what you have already written. Does your style stay the same? Have you given the readers what you promised them? Are you sticking to your table of contents? If you are making any major changes in any part of the book, be sure to keep the editor apprised of what you are actually doing.

10. Submit your book. Your contract with the publisher will tell you how to submit your manuscript. Some contracts call for the book to be submitted in stages as the sections are done. Others ask for the entire book. If you have any questions along the way, submit part of your book to your editor and ask if your material is coming along as she envisioned.

    You will normally be expected to turn in a hard copy, which again is simply the book printed, double-spaced on white 8½ by 11 inch paper, and a computer disk using a software program compatible with the publisher's programs.

11. Review the editing. You will probably get your book back one or two times after different stages of editing and/or layout. Read it carefully to be sure that no changes were made that affect the content of the material or the ideas you are trying to convey to the reader. There may be some things you want changed back. Other times, you may actually find that the editor has helped clarify a point you were trying to make. Always deal with the materials the editor sends immediately because if you miss your given deadline, you can jeopardize your book's ability to get published on time.

12. Gear up for promoting your book. Thought you could rest now? Nope. This is the important time to begin promoting your book. If your publisher has a publicist assigned to your project, start working with him or her to get the word out. This is also the time to begin any promotional activities you told the publisher you would do on your own.

    Before your book comes out, be sure that any publications or other media that might be interested have been notified in time to have their coverage of your book coincide with its publication date.

    There are several ways that publications might use information about your book. You can study previous issues to determine which approach will work best. Some magazines do book reviews or brief write-ups to inform readers about upcoming books that will interest them. Some will contract for excerpts from the book (your publicist can help you arrange this). Finally, you might write an article proposal to the magazine for an idea that is based on your book.

OK, now you can rest. But just for a minute. Your promotional activities will be critical to your book's success. If you want to gain the maximum exposure and benefit from it, you will need to plan to actively promote it, especially for the first year it is out.

WHEN YOU SHOULD CONSIDER SELF-PUBLISHING

Before energy and public policy consultant Ernest J. Oppenheimer, Ph.D., self-published *Natural Gas, the Best Energy Source,* he tried to interest a commercial publisher, but the editor at McGraw-Hill told him that he didn't think he could sell 5,000 copies of the book, which was the minimum expectation the company required to publish. The editor casually told Oppenheimer that maybe he should consider self-publishing. So he did.

Oppenheimer credits his success to careful marketing research before writing the book. "This was a very special kind of situation with a large industry providing the research and being my main customer," he says. He went to leaders in the natural gas industry and asked them questions about the book he wanted to write, everything from what would be an attractive price to whether they preferred hard or soft covers. Not surprisingly, these were also people he had targeted as being in a position to purchase large quantities (some ended up buying up to 5,000 copies each!).

As an added incentive, Oppenheimer offered to do a free lecture for companies that purchased 2,500 copies of his book and paid his travel expenses.

Before he knew it, Oppenheimer had sold 50,000 copies and the editor at McGraw-Hill was calling him to see if he'd still consider publishing with them. The answer was no. That book has already sold 85,000 copies and is continuing to do well.

Having a book published by an established publisher gives you the advantage of having experts help you with the production, promotion, and marketing of your book. All this is free to you and can be a wonderfully supportive way to help you get your message out. Your royalties will often be 10 percent to 15 percent for your part in creating the book.

However, there are times when people want more control over the book; have the energy and resources to handle all the production, promotion, and marketing necessary; and want to make more money on the project than they think they will through a commercial publisher. According to self-publishing guru Gordon Burgett, self-publishers can earn 50 percent profit from each book if they aggressively market it and have more than one key font of sales, such as bookstores and BOR (Back of the Room) sales at events. In his book, *Publishing to Niche Markets,* he discusses ways to focus tightly on your niche area of expertise in order to focus tightly on high profits.

What are the key points that make a book project a good bet for self-publishing? According to Burgett they are:

- *Targeting.* Some topics are of interest to only a relatively small audience making them uneconomical to a commercial publisher.

- *Customizing.* By controlling all the production yourself, you will be in an excellent position to be sure it is bound, illustrated, etc., exactly the way you believe it needs to be to appeal to your readers.

- *Expanding.* Just as your book is an expansion of your current business, you can continue that expansion by giving seminars on your topic (see Chapter 7), writing articles or having excerpts from your book published, or speaking on your topic (see Chapter 6).

Dollars and Sense

Before you decide to race out to become a self-publisher, be sure you have the funds available to get started.

Burgett estimates that to produce a 200-page, 6″ x 9″, perfect bound, softcover trade book without color (other than a four-color cover) and fewer than a dozen illustrations, it will cost approximately $5,000 to have 2,000 copies printed. That does not include costs you may incur for others to gather information or for permission to use material that has been copyrighted by others.

If you also add production costs for getting your manuscript disk-ready you could be looking at a total expense from $7,000 to $9,000. However, since each book is an individual project and different people have different skills they can use to minimize the expenses, you may be able to publish more affordably than that.

Another great resource if you are considering self-publishing is Tom and Marilyn Ross' book, *The Complete Guide to Self-Publishing*. This thick volume covers everything you wanted to know and a lot you couldn't even imagine to ask about self-publishing. One great chapter that deserves special attention by anyone new to self-publishing is their chapter on subsidy (vanity) publishers.

Subsidy publishers are companies that offer to publish books when you, the author, pay all the bills. The Rosses note that charges can range from $4,000 to more than $25,000 depending on the size of your book and the quantity you want printed. These companies often have contracts that tie up your rights to your book and they can even charge you to purchase copies of the book you already paid to have published! This is not a prestigious way to get your book into print. Most bookstores do not stock books from these publishers and reputable reviewers often pitch them in the trash can unread.

Self-publishing, on the other hand, is a respected way to get into print, although it is a lot of work for you. If you are considering this option, be sure to read the two books mentioned earlier and, if possible, attend a workshop offered by these authors to be sure you clearly understand the pros and cons.

As you can see, there are may ways you can write for publication to build your business. People just like you do it every day and gain the benefits. You can be next. Start by completing the following self-survey for articles and/or the self-survey for books.

SELF-SURVEY: WORKSHEET FOR PLANNING A WRITING PROJECT

Articles

Goals I hope to achieve through writing articles for publication:

_____

_____

Topic I want to write about: _____

Who will read it: _____

Where will they find it: _____

Who is the editor I need to write to: _____

Magazine address: _____

Telephone/fax numbers: _____

Experts I need to contact for information and quotes:_____

_____

Name/Telephone: _____

Date called and results: _____

Date query letter sent: _____

Date followed up with editor: _____

Date article due to editor: _____

Anticipated publication date: _____

Results of having article published (for example, new clients or calls from the media): _____

_____

_____

_____

SELF-SURVEY: WORKSHEET FOR PLANNING A WRITING PROJECT

Books

Goals I hope to achieve through writing books for publication:

_____

_____

Topic I want to write about: _____

Who will read it: _____

Where will they find it: _____

Books that are competitive with mine: _____

_____

Publishers that do books similar to mine: _____

_____

Publisher that seems best: _____

Name of editor at that publisher: _____

Key points to make in the proposal: _____

_____

Dates proposal elements completed: _____

    Overview with selling hook: _____

    Sample chapter: _____

    Outline: _____

    Author information: _____

    Other materials: _____

Date proposal sent: _____

Result: _____

_____

_____

6

Yes, You Can Say
a Few Words

In all probability, there are few things you enjoy talking about more than your business. Your customers, your friends, even your relatives have undoubtedly heard a lot about your professional triumphs. But have you ever considered speaking to audiences about what you do and what your business offers?

Just the thought of public speaking frightens some people. Surveys have shown that it is the most scary thing that many people can imagine. Yet, it doesn't have to be so intimidating. Many people speak regularly to a wide range of audiences and you can, too.

The secret to public speaking is to prepare. Find the right audience. Write a speech that gives them information they can use. Then deliver it with conviction.

After all, you have a wealth of knowledge about your business. Think about all the people who would benefit from even a fraction of the knowledge you have! With a little planning and practice, you will be in the position of being a speaker who is much sought-after by the very people who would make wonderful customers and clients.

Isadora Alman, MFCC, is a board-certified sexologist who specializes in communication and relationship issues. When she was beginning her practice in San Francisco, California, she decided to build her name recognition by giving speeches to fraternal and social organizations. She says, "I rarely saw a direct link between my speaking and getting new clients, but the more I spoke, the more clients I got!"

GETTING HELP TO GET STARTED

What if you are really uncomfortable with the idea of giving a speech, but you recognize the value that giving speeches can add to your business and career? There are resources you can access to help you gain the skills you need to be a confident speaker.

Perhaps the best known resource is Toastmasters International. Based in Rancho Santa Margarita, California, this organization offers members assistance at improving their public speaking skills and increasing their leadership and management skills.

As a Toastmaster, you will belong to a local club in your area. Each meeting includes prepared speeches from members, impromptu speeches from members, oral evaluations of the prepared speeches, as well as reports from other people who are evaluating the speeches for aspects such as grammar, timing, counting repetitive speech patterns, etc.

Members are given opportunities to give a number of different styles of speeches including those that demonstrate vocal variety, working with words, being persuasive, speaking with knowledge, and inspiring the audience. Fortunately for those who need some time to get accustomed to the concepts before they stand up and speak, you can take your time and decide when you are ready to participate. You are not required to start your speeches at any specific time in your membership.

As you gain experience and expertise in speaking, Toastmasters also offers designations you can earn and contests you can win.

The cost of being in Toastmasters (at this writing) is very economical, especially compared to hiring a speaking coach to help you. There is a $16 initiation fee (for materials) plus eighteen dollars every six months and any dues your local club assesses. See the Resources section for contact information.

How much can Toastmasters help you? Hans G. Rohl knows. When the firm he works for, Klein & Barenblat, was invited to speak on property tax valuation at the San Antonio Chapter of the Texas Society of CPA's, the firm's principals chose Rohl to give the presentation because they knew of his three-year involvement with Toastmasters. With seven months to prepare his speech, Rohl reluctantly accepted. Five months later, he was pleading to be released from the assignment because his nerves were getting the better of him.

Because this was a prestigious opportunity for the firm, his boss let him know that he had the choice of either keeping his commitment or resigning. So Rohl collected the data he needed, wrote and rewrote his speech, and practiced it over and over again.

Fully expecting disaster to strike, Rohl stepped to the front of the room and faced the sixty attendees who had come to hear his forty-five minute presentation. And guess what? It went beautifully! Within hours, his firm had acquired a valuable new contract from one of the attendees and that was just the start of the new business that was generated because of his speech.

Now, when Rohl looks back on that day, he credits Toastmasters with giving him the experience, insight, and skills to make this presentation work so well. He has even started thinking about giving more seminars in the future!

So, if you are nervous about talking in front of a group, take a tip from Rohl and check out your local Toastmasters group. It can open doors to ways you can promote yourself and your business that you would never have dreamed of otherwise.

FINDING THE RIGHT AUDIENCE

The first consideration you have in planning your speaking program is your audience. Who will it be? Who should it be? Obviously, if your business is a daycare center, you want to talk to groups that are primarily made up of parents of young children.

If your business is in interior decorating, your best audiences could be people who have recently moved or purchased a new home. If your business is auto detailing, you will want to talk to people who take pride in their cars.

Take a sheet of paper and answer these questions:

✓ Who is my customer?
  - Are my customers primarily male or female?
  - What is their age group?
  - What unique characteristics do they have as a group?
✓ What groups do my customers belong to?
  - What community groups are they active in?
  - What service groups (for example, Elks, Soroptomists) are they active in?
  - What professional groups?
  - What business groups?
✓ Where else do they go to hear people speak?
  - Local college and university courses?
  - Community recreational courses?
  - Other?

The best places to look for speaking engagements are probably right in your town. All sorts of groups have regular meetings and their program planners are always searching for people who can share interesting information with the group.

You might want to start with groups where you are already a member. You have the advantage of knowing how the meetings usually go and having a very supportive audience. Then branch out and contact other small groups (to start) and offer to speak at their meetings.

You will need to come up with one or more topics you feel comfortable speaking about so that you can propose them to the program planners. At first, you might want to just pick one area of interest about your business (such as tax planning for a CPA) and then be willing to customize it for each audience. For instance, that same speech on tax planning would probably be slightly different for people who have businesses that include a lot of employees and inventory than for a group of consultants who have neither employees nor substantial inventory.

Remember that the reason most people listen to a speech is to gather information they can use to make their own lives better. One easy way to create a speech is by organizing tips on one specific area of your expertise. You might have a title like, "Five Ways to … " or "Seven Secrets of …." If your industry is going through a period of controversy, you might find audiences very interested in a speech that looks at the issue from an insider's perspective.

Getting Booked

If you are dealing with local organizations and you are known in your community, you may be able to get "booked" (scheduled to give a talk) by just making a few phone calls. If you are not yet known to the program planner, you might start by sending him or her a letter offering your services. Your letter should start out with an exciting opening sentence that makes the program planner want to know more about you and your subject. Tell the planner what benefits your speech will have for the audience and why you are just the expert they need to hear. Finally, say that you will be in touch in a week to see if they have any questions and then do it!

It is a good idea to include some materials with your letter to help the program planner realize that you are capable of providing the attendees with a good speech full of solid information. Those materials might include the following:

- Articles you wrote that have been published on the subject
- Articles quoting you as an expert on the subject
- Brochures from your business
- A brief resume focusing on your expertise in this topic
- An audiotape (if the quality is good) of you delivering a similar speech to an audience
- Letter(s) of thanks from other organizations where you have spoken

Don't feel that you need to send all of the materials, but if you have some of them, they will reassure the program planner about your abilities to deliver a great speech.

If the volume of material you have to send becomes a handful (anything over five sheets), it is a good idea to send it in a presentation folder. Pick folders that are attractive and have one or two large pockets inside to hold the papers. Some folders also have a place on the pocket to mount one of your business cards. If you have folders that have been made up for your business and have your logo or company name on them, so much the better. Sending the materials in a folder looks more professional and helps the recipient keep your materials together.

Absolute No-No's

Remember that while you are giving the group some wonderful information they can use, you are also promoting yourself and your business. All your dealings with the organization must be of the highest caliber or your professional reputation will suffer.

There are two areas where people can cause themselves problems: ethics and manners.

Obviously, if the CPA mentioned earlier told people stories about all the falsified tax returns he'd gotten through the IRS, everyone in the room would assume his services would be ethically suspect. So present yourself at your best so that your speech will enhance, not destroy your reputation.

Another potential problem area arises when people expect to be treated like prima donnas. You should act more like an eager employee than a rock star. Don't bring a guest with you unless you have asked the program chair if you can (especially if the group is hosting you to a meal). Don't expect to be served better food than the others. Never drink alcohol before your speech. You may think it will relax you, but it actually will take away your edge and when used to excess, can result in embarrassment for you and your hosts.

It is best to act like the professional you are. Plan to get there a little early to check and make sure that you have what you need in terms of a lectern, projectors, microphones, and so on. Whenever possible, test the electronic devices to be sure they actually work. Be gracious to the people representing your host organization, and be warm and friendly to the attendees.

Finally, don't expect to be paid—at least in the beginning. Most local groups are happy to buy you a meal if their meetings include meals for members. Occasionally, there may be a modest honorarium in the twenty, fifty, or one hundred dollar range. If there is, the group will generally offer it to you. Novice speakers who ask for money, frequently do not get the booking. As you gain experience as a speaker, you may find that someone who heard you speak at one function is in a position to help you get a booking at a larger function that may pay. Professional speakers who make a living at their craft have often started just as you are, but their focus was on promoting themselves as a speaker while you are more likely focusing on promoting your business through your speaking.

Another Avenue

Depending on the business goals you have set for yourself, you also might look to your profession's conferences and conventions as a place to give speeches. One excellent way to establish yourself as an expert is to give papers or sit on panels at these events.

In many fields, especially those dealing with engineering, science, and medicine, conferences offer practitioners opportunities to do what is called presenting a paper. This process starts when you read the "call for papers" in organizational writings. The call will list the kinds of topics the conference will cover and give you details about how you submit a proposal. If you don't know when those calls are issued, contact the national office of the organization for details.

When your proposal is accepted, you will generally be expected to write a paper that you will present. This paper may include charts or other graphics that you should copy onto clear sheets for overhead projection (most good copy shops can do it if you do not have the capability). At the conference, you will be assigned a room and a time and other attendees will come to hear you read your paper and possibly further explain the points you are trying to make. Be prepared for questions from audience members. If you are not comfortable being interrupted, it is perfectly acceptable to state that you will take questions only at the end of your presentation.

An easier way to gain recognition as an expert at your industry's conferences and conventions is to sit on a panel in a discussion. Panelists are often expected to speak for anywhere from a few minutes to half an hour (check with the moderator before the event). You are less likely to be expected to bring visual aids than if you were giving a paper. The challenging part of being on a panel is that you are quite likely to be asked a number of questions by attendees. This can be difficult for some people. However, remember that all the attendees are there because they are interested in your topic and hope to learn something new. If you look at it as an opportunity to share what you know with new friends, you may find it a very enjoyable experience!

WRITING AN EFFECTIVE SPEECH

Even the most fascinating topic in the world won't keep the audience awake if the speech itself is boring. You need to expect to spend many hours writing (and rewriting) your speech before you give it.

There are many styles of writing speeches and you may need to try several before you decide what is best for you. Some people like to create an outline and then write the speech. The benefit to this style is that you can tightly structure your talk and be sure to cover all the important points. If you choose this style, expect to spend a lot of time working on the outline because that will provide the structure for your talk.

Some people like to do more of a stream of consciousness style of writing. They sit down in front of their computers or use pads of paper and just start writing everything that comes to mind. If you decide to use this technique, you will spend a lot of time reworking your speech because it is unlikely that you will create a coherent structure on the first try. It will be interesting to try the different elements of the speech in different orders to change the feeling and tempo of the talk.

Others start with a tape recorder. If you are not comfortable with your writing style or if it tends to be stilted and unnatural sounding when read aloud, record yourself talking about your topic for at least twice as long as your speech is supposed to last. Then transcribe it onto paper or a computer disk. There are secretarial services that will do this fairly economically. If you don't know of one, your copy shop or print shop should be able to give you a referral.

The reason to speak for a longer period than your speech will last is so you can edit your speech. The goal is to capture your best material and to keep your talk energetic and exciting. Once you have the speech on paper or disk, edit and arrange it much like the people who started by writing it down.

You have undoubtedly heard that you should start your speech with a joke. Not true. Unless you have an original story that relates directly to your topic, starting with a joke can be deadly. Also, if the story/joke is well known already in your industry, you may actually hear people groan or tell the punch line along with you.

One of the best ways to start your speech is with an exciting example of the benefit that the audience will gain from the information you have to offer. After all, which would be more likely to get your attention, "A funny thing happened to me on the way to this meeting ... " or "When Kevin Garrison came to hear me speak a year ago, his business was in danger of failing financially. Less than six months later, he had used the techniques I'm going to teach you today to double his sales and increase his profits"?

How should you plot out your speech? To paraphrase a well-known technique, "First you tell them what you're going to tell them. Then you tell them. Then you review what you've told them." Repeating your core information three times in different ways can help cement it in your audience's minds.

Do not try to tell the audience everything you learned about your business over your entire career. Not only is it impossible, you will probably just overload them with information and they are not likely to go away with any new knowledge they can actually use.

It is best to cover a few points (probably three to five) that are crucial for your audience. Then cover those points thoroughly. It can help if you can give those points catchy names that you use repeatedly in the speech to make your point. Those names will help the audience remember your most important points.

TECHNIQUES FOR MAKING YOUR SPEECH LIVELY, ENTERTAINING, AND INFORMATIVE

There are some techniques you can use that will make your speech touch your audience in a way that will excite and fascinate them and even touch them emotionally.

One critical fact to remember is that people learn in different ways. Sight, sound, even touch are ways that people receive and process information. If all you do is stand there and talk, you are really only giving them sound, and studies have shown that people learn about five times as much by seeing things as they do by hearing them.

Visual Images Reinforce Your Message

So what can you do to help your audience remember more of your speech? Use visual aids. Projecting visuals like photos and charts onto a screen is a time-proven way of helping reinforce the message you are providing.

When you use this technique be sure you have enough different images to keep things moving. Practice using the visuals with your speech until you are comfortable working with the words and images together. Also, practice using the visuals in a room as large as the one where you will be giving the speech. While you are doing this practice, make sure the people sitting in the back of the room will be able to see your visuals. Walk "to the back of the room." Can you still see the words and images on the screen clearly? If you can't then neither will your audience. You will need to fix or re-do your visuals.

Make the Human Connection

People love to hear stories about other people. They also identify with stories about people who are dealing with situations that are similar to the ones they face themselves. You can help your audience remember the critical points in your speech by illustrating them with stories that put a human face on the problem.

Plan carefully when you decide which stories to use. They should always be clear examples of the point you want to make. It can be tempting to include extraneous facts in the story just because you found them interesting, but in a speech, they are more likely to distract from your message.

When you are using stories about real people, be careful not to disclose facts about them that are not public record unless you have their written permission.

Put It in Their Hands

Even when your audience members are taking copious notes during your speech, you can reinforce your message with carefully crafted handouts. Depending on the topic and style of your speech, your handouts could be an outline or agenda sheet, worksheets for them to fill out, or even small gifts. If you want to hand out written copies of your speech, wait until the end of your talk so that audience members are paying attention to you and not sitting there reading your handout.

Looking Good

As the old saying goes, "You never get a second chance to make a good first impression." When you arrive at the site where you are going to give your speech, people will begin to make decisions about you based on how you look and handle yourself.

There are several keys to making a great visual impression:

 Dress appropriately. How you dress will depend on what is appropriate for your profession and what is appropriate for the group and the place where they meet. For instance, if you own a health club and are talking about the benefits of exercise, you could wear a suit or other business wear. However, the same person giving a speech that includes a demonstration of different exercises should wear clothing appropriate for exercising. While the business wear is appropriate almost anywhere, the exercise clothes would be more acceptable at a meeting in a social hall or clubroom than in an upscale restaurant.

Be comfortable. If your shirt collar is too tight, your skirt too short, or you are worried about gaps developing between the buttons of your outfit, you will certainly not be able to give your audience your full attention. When you are planning your outfit, be sure to think about the shoes you will wear and whether you can stand for extended periods in those shoes without discomfort.

Keep it simple. Unless your speech involves costumes (cowboy outfit if you own a store of Western wear or clown outfit if you do children's parties), it is best to keep your outfit simple. It makes a classy visual impression and helps draw attention to you and your talk instead of your clothes.

Accessorize carefully. If you have ever tried to listen to a speech, but were constantly distracted by the clink of bracelets against each other or tinkling sounds from earrings with dangling ornaments that hit each other everytime the speaker moved, you know why it is important to plan your accessories carefully. Jewelry that reflects light can also distract the audience from your message. A day or two before you give your talk, try on your entire outfit with the accessories. Move around in front of a mirror. Are the accessories flattering you or are they drawing your eyes away from your face? When in doubt go without.

Makeup tips. Remember that your audience will not be seeing you as close as you see your mirror when you are putting on makeup. In order for you to look your best in front of the room, you may need to adjust your makeup so that your eye and lip colors are stronger than normal. Experiment by putting on your makeup and looking in a mirror from across the room. Does your face stand out or fade away? If you are having difficulty finding a look you are comfortable with, there are beauty consultants at makeup counters in department stores or as independent distributors for some brand products such as Avon and Mary Kay who can help you find a successful look. Be sure to wear the makeup for a day before you give your speech in case it gives you problems after you have been wearing it for a while.

A quick note for the men reading this. Makeup for men is becoming more acceptable, especially in situations where appearances are important. If you are not comfortable with the way you look, consider having an image consultation. You may find that a light dusting of powder for a sweaty brow makes you much more comfortable in front of a group.

How to Guarantee a Great Introduction

What do you want the audience to know about you before you start your speech? Well, don't count on the program chair of the group to know what that is and use it in the introduction. You need to prepare an introduction for him or her to read to be absolutely certain that you get the introduction you want.

Why not just trust the introducer to remember the facts you told him or her and to do a good job? Sometimes you will get an excellent introduction that way. However, it is more likely that there will be errors in the facts the introducer remembers, he or she may tell a joke that bombs, or will go on endlessly (using too much of the time allowed to you), or, conversely, the introducer will barely say more than your name.

Your introduction should be no longer than one page (typed and double-spaced). It should tell the audience who you are, what your topic is, and why you are an expert on this topic. If you have an affiliation with the organization, it can be nice to mention it in the introduction because it helps develop a positive bond between you and the audience even before you start your talk.

Author and speaker consultant Lilly Walters of the Walters International Speakers Bureau gives some elegantly simple ways to guarantee a great introduction in her book, *Secrets of Successful Speakers*. She advises you to send your introducer a copy of the introduction at least a few days before your talk and then bring a copy with you. As she notes, Murphy's Law dictates that the introducer will have your carefully crafted introduction back at his or her office and will need a fresh copy at the event.

Walters also includes notes on the bottom of her introduction for the person reading it. Her notes remind the introducer to face her and start the applause as she walks in, wait for her at the lectern, extend his or her hand to great her as she approaches the lectern, and even reminds the introducer to leave the lectern after the handshake.

That may sound like a lot of detail, but most people are more comfortable if they know what is expected of them, so her directions are appreciated.

Use Your Speech to Develop New Sales

Now that you have developed and given your wonderful speech, you will want to be sure that you benefit from it as much as the audience. There are several ways that you can turn your audience into customers or clients:

Bring Products to Sell.   Arrange with the program chair for you to set up a table at the back of the room where you can sell your products before or after the speech.

Collect Business Cards.   If possible, make a note on the back of each one about what you talked about with the person who gave you the card. Later that day or the next, write each person a brief note thanking them for talking with you and giving them any information you said you would get for them.

Have a Raffle.   Offer a product or service to the organization to be raffled off. Then supply the organization with entry forms for the raffle that require each participant to write down his or her name, address, and telephone number on the form (perhaps provide room on the form for any questions the participant may have for you). Alternatively, in a business setting, have everyone put their business card in the pot. Draw a card out and make a presentation of the award. You now have contact information about all these people who have already demonstrated an interest in what you have to offer! Be sure to follow up by sending them brochures or fliers making a special offer to get them started as customers and clients.

IMAGINE WHERE THE FUTURE CAN LEAD YOU

In the beginning of this chapter, Isadora Alman described how giving speeches helped build her practice as a therapist. But that was only part of the benefit. As she gave more speeches, she was more and more in demand. It led to a regular radio program on KRQR, which provided her with new clients for years. She has even appeared on a number of television shows at a regional and national level.

All of her public speaking was helping her business, building a professional image, and even creating a little fame. Alman remembers, "Shortly after I got the radio show, I was having dinner in a San Francisco restaurant. Suddenly a waiter came up and asked if I was Isadora Alman. He had had his back to me and recognized my voice. That made me feel really famous!"

Speaking about your business can have many wonderful benefits for you, too. All you need to do is get started!

SELF-SURVEY: WORKSHEET FOR DEVELOPING A SPEAKING PROGRAM

What are the goals I hope to achieve through speaking? ____

_____

_____

Topic I want to speak about: _____

Groups in which members are likely to be interested: _____

_____

Name of program chair and date contacted: _____

_____

Date(s) scheduled to speak: _____

Title of speech: _____

Length: _____

Name and telephone of contact person: _____

_____

Equipment needed and how it will be acquired: _____

_____

_____

Handouts I plan to bring: _____

Quantity: _____

Door prize or raffle prize I plan to bring: _____

Merchandise I plan to bring to sell at the back of the room:

_____

Results of giving speech: _____

_____

Referrals for giving other talks I got from attendees: _____

_____

_____

7

Sell It with a Seminar

Whether your business deals in products or services, you can benefit from teaching people through seminars, adult education programs, and other outlets where adults go to learn skills to enrich their professional and personal lives.

The seminars and workshops you give can be anywhere from half a day to a few days to a week or more. They will require more preparation and more and better materials than those you need for speeches, so this is a step up in terms of the commitment you need to make to be successful.

If you think that the market for seminars and workshops is small, you need to realize that according to Howard L. Shenson's book, *How to Develop and Promote Successful Seminars and Workshops,* approximately 80 percent of the adults in the United States will have attended one or more public seminars and workshops by the year 2010.

Teaching classes or seminars offers you spectacular opportunities to establish yourself as an expert and attract potential new clients and customers. In fact, in Shenson's book, he states that research shows that one out of every nine seminar attendees becomes a client for consulting services when the seminar leader is skilled.

CHOOSING A FORMAT AND A TOPIC

Depending on your personal goals, you can offer anything from an academic-style class that gives technical information to a demonstration-style class that gives students hands-on experience in an area they want to learn more about.

Examples of potential seminar or class topics include:

- Local area computer networks (if you are a computer consultant)
- Consumer law (if you are a consumer attorney)
- Keys to successful direct marketing (if you own a direct marketing company)
- Natural pain relief (if you are a chiropractor or acupuncturist)
- Achieve wealth by reducing clutter (if you are an organizational consultant)
- Eat to live (if you are a nutritionist or psychotherapist who works with people who have eating disorders)
- Making holiday decorations (if you have a craft store)
- How to create a saltwater aquarium (if you have a pet store)

CREATE CLASSES THAT PROMOTE YOUR PRODUCTS OR SERVICES

People are always interested in learning, and people who make their subjects interesting and fun are always in demand. Especially if you are considering offering classes or seminars that people sign up for voluntarily, as opposed to being required to attend for employment reasons, be sure to keep the fun factor in mind. In fact, the Learning Annex, which offers a wide range of classes in many major cities, reminds people in its literature that "School was never like this!"

How different are Learning Annex classes from the classes you took in school? Well, classes listed from a recent catalog include "Terminator Craps, Learn Tips from a Gambling Expert,"

"Aphrodisiacs: Learn Ayurvedic Secrets to Ignite Your Sex Life," or "Angels: How to Have an Angelic Encounter." Although you might not want to teach those classes, many of the Learning Annex's classes are taught by businesspeople, just like you, who have something to share and who hope to promote their businesses. Some of the courses offered by business owners in that same catalog included a certified, licensed massage therapist who taught "Massage for Couples"; a real estate broker who taught "How to Buy and Sell a Fixer-Upper"; a builder of coin laundries who taught "Clean Up in the Coin Laundry Business"; and a travel industry consultant who taught "The Art of Discount Travel."

As you consider topics you might teach, think of your seminar as giving people a taste of your expertise that will leave them wanting more. Most adults hope to take away a few facts or skills they can use from a class; they don't expect to duplicate your level of expertise from your seminars.

Think about what skills you can teach that will be especially attractive to others. There are some areas that tend to always be in high demand:

- Money—How to get it and how to keep it
- Relationships—Everything from love matches to dealing with children and coworkers
- Spirituality—Traditional to new age
- Careers—How to choose a career and get ahead
- Travel—Where to go and how to get there
- The Arts—Performing and understanding
- Health—Everything from fitness to healing

Review the above list. In all likelihood, you can come up with class ideas that would fall under several of the general topics given. On a separate sheet of paper, make a list of the ideas that come to mind by category. Then, next to each idea, list the kinds of people who would be interested in the class and how they could benefit your business. An example for someone who has a health food store would look like this:

Money: Low Cost Health Meals
Budget-conscious consumers
Young adults
Bring in new customers who are interested in saving
money and getting good nutrition

Travel: "Cooking with the Grains of the World"
Sophisticated consumers
Ethnically diverse customers
Attract customers who normally shop at gourmet shops
or ethnic markets

Health: "Fighting Allergies at the Dinner Table"
People dealing with food allergies
Become a resource for people who are searching for
wholesome, natural foods

Notice that each of the seminar titles clearly tells the prospective student what the benefit of attending this seminar will be. Sometimes you can add a little humor ("And the Beat Goes On … Eating for a Healthy Heart") or alliteration ("How to Have a Healthy Heart"). Just be sure that when people read or hear your title they will have a clear idea of what you plan to teach. Otherwise, they won't sign up at all.

OPPORTUNITIES TO BE PAID TO SHARE YOUR EXPERTISE AND PROMOTE YOUR BUSINESS

While some people aggressively pursue a career in public speaking and teaching as a major source of income, you should not expect to get rich from your seminars alone—at least not in the beginning.

That does not mean you should not expect to be paid in some manner. One way to look at the pay issue is that any opportunity you get to talk to others about your business is an opportunity to gain new customers and clients. This indirect benefit of giving a seminar can have very exciting ramifications for your business.

In your local area, check into the adult education programs through the community, school district, or college or university. Your payment through these organizations will either be a percentage of the gate (fees collected from attendees) or, in the case of a college or university, it may be a flat fee based on the number of hours you teach the course.

At least during your initial attempts, you will probably find it more convenient to teach through another organization like a university extension program, a community adult education program, or as part of a professional conference. When you teach for such organizations, they will be responsible for handling all the details from acquiring the site to advertising and registering students. Make no mistake, there is a lot of work involved in those tasks and a substantial financial risk. If you're considering giving seminars and workshops independently at some time, try giving them through an organization first to reduce your risks. Also, before the temptation to make all the money on the workshops bites you, remember that unless giving seminars is your only business, it may take too much time away from your primary business. You won't look like much of a success when teaching if your basic business went bankrupt.

If you really enjoy speaking and teaching, you may want to continue to pursue this at a professional level. Here the fees can easily be many thousands of dollars for a talk or seminar. Again, this level of involvement as a speaker can take your attention away from your primary business if you are not careful.

If you want to pursue speaking as a profession, start by getting a lot of experience as a seminar leader at your local level. Read *Speak and Grow Rich* by Dottie and Lilly Walters. This comprehensive book will give you real insight into the benefits, drawbacks, and effort required to become a professional speaker.

NUTS AND BOLTS OF PUTTING ON YOUR OWN CLASS OR SEMINAR

The first question you need to ask yourself when you are considering putting on a class or seminar is, What do I know that others will pay to learn? You may want to teach something that is marvelously fascinating to you, but no one else really cares about. The best way to come up with a seminar idea is take a piece of paper and make a list of the questions people ask you about your work. Do this exercise without worrying about having too many questions or whether you even think a question would make good seminar material.

Once you are done, look at the list again. Which questions can you rewrite by putting them into several categories? Do it.

Now, which categories have the most questions? These are probably areas that many people have asked you about because they feel they impact on their own lives.

As you study the two or three most detailed categories, you will probably start having an idea of what kind of class you could teach that would provide the information requested in those questions.

Developing Your Class

Once you have chosen a topic for your class, it is time to think about where people would look for it. If it is a basic class, perhaps on health care, people might look for it in adult education courses offered by the local school district. If it is a more technical topic that would help people with their career advancement, they might look for it in a university extension program. If it is something for fun, personal development, or curiosity, like personal relationship or new age topics, they might be more likely to look for it in an independent adult learning program like the Learning Annex.

Do *not* limit yourself based on these broad categories. Check with organizations that offer classes. Ask for copies of their most recent catalogs and look through them. Is someone already teaching the class you want to teach? Can you develop your idea so you are teaching a complementary rather than competing class? Does the catalog offer classes that would appeal to the same people you think will be interested in your class?

Once you have chosen a venue, look at the catalog again and see how long the classes tend to run. They could last anywhere from one evening or one full day to a semester of one-hour classes.

Make an outline of what you would expect to teach during your class. Remember, you don't have to be talking every minute, your students will be asking questions. You also may want to include some individual and group activities, where appropriate, as they can help with the learning process.

Think about the different ways people learn. Some are most comfortable learning through hearing a lecture, others absorb more information when there are great visuals to explain the information, still others learn best with a hands-on approach.

What can you do in your class to help people with each of these different learning styles? What equipment will you need to accomplish this goal? Many venues will supply equipment like slide projectors, overhead projectors, microphones, etc., but they need to know in advance so they can include these items in their budget projections.

Will you test your students to evaluate how much they learned? How often will tests be given? If the course is through a university extension program, will you need to grade students? If so, what will you base those grades on?

After you have thought through all this information, you will need to write a class proposal document. In it give the decision makers at the institution where you want to teach all the information they will need to decide if your class will fill the needs of their students. Information they will need includes your outline, equipment needs, and possibly a few paragraphs about who you believe your students will be and how the class will help them.

Before you send the document, call the organization and ask for the correct name (including spelling and gender) of the person to whom you should send class proposals. Then write a brief cover letter to that person explaining that you would like to propose a class. If you have had any experience in speaking or teaching the proposed subject, mention it in the letter. Attach a copy of your class proposal to the cover letter. If you have any letters of recommendation from people or sponsoring groups where you have spoken on this topic, include a photocopy of the letter. Also, if it will strengthen you package, send a copy of your current resume.

Approximately five to ten days after the person should have received your package, call to verify that it arrived. You also can ask the person if he or she has any questions. Do not start out by conducting a sales call that will sell them your class—your documents should do that for you. However, if the person has questions about your class or your expertise, answer his or her questions.

Once an institution has decided to offer your class, someone there will call you to schedule it. Remember that once you have agreed to a date or dates, the person will schedule space for you and advertise the date in the catalog. You may not be able to change the date once you have agreed to it. If you cannot teach the class on that schedule, your only option may be to cancel the class, and this will not go over well with the institution if it has already invested money in space rental and catalog expenses.

The institution will usually send you contracts to sign outlining the support services it will supply for your class and how much (and when) you will be paid. You will need to return these documents promptly.

If you are fortunate, the institution also will either ask you to write your catalog copy (the description of your class and your personal qualifications) or review the copy they have written. The reason you want to do this is to be sure that the catalog copy accurately reflects what you hope to teach so that the students will come with realistic expectations.

Delivering Value to Your Students

One mistake novice teachers sometimes make when they offer a class that is intended to promote their careers is that they try too hard to sell the students into becoming clients and customers.

Your goal in teaching is to share information in such a way that it establishes your competence in the subject matter. If you keep saying, "Call my secretary Monday and make an appointment so we can go over your situation in more detail," the students will feel cheated. They paid to have you teach them something; they expect value for their money.

On the other hand, it is perfectly acceptable to put your business name, address, and telephone number on handouts you give your students in class. You also can use your past experiences as examples of the points you want to teach, as long as telling those stories will not violate client confidentiality. Many educational outlets will also be agreeable to your giving a brief pitch for your business at the close of class. If you are not sure exactly how much self-promotion is acceptable at the venue where you are teaching, ask the person there who is coordinating your class setup.

Be a Good Presenter

Spend some time looking over your course outline and making notes for yourself. Don't assume that just because you are comfortable talking one-on-one to clients and customers that you are ready to teach a class. In teaching a class, you need to be relating to a number of people at the same time. You will want to create a balance of giving information, asking questions, and answering questions from your students.

One good tip is to create a schedule of what information you want to be imparting to your students at what point in the class. Then check your schedule throughout the class time; if you are falling behind, try to get back on schedule without missing any of the critically important information. If you don't pace yourself, you may reach the end of the class period and not have covered everything your catalog copy promised—and your students will be understandably upset.

Learn How to Do Better Next Time

Nearly every good speaker tries to learn more about how the audience perceives them and how they can do a better job next time. One way you can do that is by having the students fill out an evaluation form at the end of the class. Some programs will supply evaluation forms, but you may have to supply your own. If the program does supply forms, just have the students complete those. Filling out several sets of evaluation forms quickly becomes a burden and the students are less likely to give detailed answers.

Following is an example of an evaluation form. Modify it to meet your needs.

EVALUATION FORM

What did you expect to learn at this class/workshop? _____

_____

_____

Did it meet your expectations? _____

What area was most helpful to you? _____

_____

Were there any areas that disappointed you? Which were they and why were they disappointing? _____

_____

_____

_____

Are there any topics you would like to see covered in a future class? _____

_____

_____

Would you be interested in a follow-up class at a later time to help with ongoing projects? _____

Would you recommend this class to a colleague?

_____

Any comments you would like to add? _____

_____

_____

Please return to:

Your name

Your address

Your fax number, if appropriate

Professionalism Pays

Finally, remember that you should present a professional image in all your dealings with your class. Go back and reread the sections in Chapter 6 that discuss how to impart that image.

Also, be sure to arrive at each class session in plenty of time to be sure the classroom is completely set up and ready. Your students may come dressed casually and with a relaxed attitude, but they are expecting you to be the professional in the room. At some level, all of them will be evaluating you and whether you are the kind of professional they would want to approach, so be sure you show yourself at your best.

When You Don't Know the Answer

No matter how much of an expert you are in your area, there will come a time when someone will ask you a question during your seminar or workshop and you just don't have the answer right then. This is not a good time to make up an answer and move on. You will appear unprofessional.

When those tough questions emerge, it is best if you ask the student for name and telephone number (or business card) and write the question on the same paper. Tell the student you will get back to him or her within the week or at the next class meeting with the answer—and then do it. No one expects you to know everything, but it will enhance your standing as a professional if you are willing to get the answer for the student. It will also increase the likelihood that the students will see you as a professional they want to do business with if they believe you will go the extra mile for them.

Think of Your Student's Comfort

No one learns well if they are uncomfortable, and as the seminar leader, it is your job to make the attendees as comfortable as possible.

Before the class, notice the room temperature. Is it comfortable for the way people are dressed? After all, a room temperature that is comfortable for people wearing suits and sweaters is going to be too cold for people dressed in lighter summer clothing. On the other hand, a room that is pleasantly warm when you begin a class can be stifling hot by the time people have been in it a few hours or if the sun has been beaming in through the windows for a while. In either case, if you suspect the temperature is going to be a problem, be sure you either know how to adjust the thermostat or how to get in touch with a maintenance person who can.

Another comfort problem that novice seminar presenters sometimes have is remembering to give people frequent breaks to use the restrooms, get coffee, or just stretch. Even the most fascinating speaker can only hold people's attention for just so long. In most cases, you should stop for a brief break every hour. If you have a 3-hour class, it is acceptable to have one 15-minute break halfway through unless you notice that the class is getting restless, in which case you should take a break sooner. You may want to schedule two 10-minute breaks during the three-hour class rather than one 15-minute break.

Selling Materials to Your Students

There may be times when you want or need to sell materials to your students. Some of these occasions can be when:

1. You have made a lot of handouts and want to recoup your expenses.
2. There are materials that students will need to participate fully (for example, food and/or specific implements in a cooking class), and you want to be sure everyone is working with the same quality and quantity of materials.
3. You have written a book and/or made audiotapes or videotapes that your students are likely to want to purchase to reinforce the things they have learned at your seminar.

When you want to sell items to students, you need to get permission from the person who is scheduling your seminar if you are going through an established community program or university extension. The institution may have a policy that you cannot sell anything that has not been preapproved by them or that was not listed as a materials fee in the catalog.

When the expenses are relatively minor, such as photocopying, the institution may offer to do it themselves and save you the costs. When the costs are for materials that will be completely used in the process of teaching the course, the institution may be happy to have you determine a dollar amount for each student. Be sure to ask the person coordinating the class if the money will be collected when the students register or if you will be expected to collect it in the first class. If you have to collect money, make sure you have some extra money to make change for people who have large bills.

Books and tapes fall into a category that professionals call BOR (back of the room sales). This is when you set up a table (often at the back of the room) to sell items. People who do this frequently will develop a whole product line that can also include posters, software, newsletter subscriptions, and books or materials by others when such materials support the message the speaker is imparting.

If you do BORs, you will want to have someone else stay at the table at all times because your students are likely to want to look at the materials (and hopefully purchase them) before class, during breaks, and after class. Be prepared to answer questions about or describe the materials to your clients/students so your helper can handle the financial transactions. You also will want to make sure you can take a break and use the restroom, which will be impossible if you are running the seminar and handling the BOR table.

If you decide to sell books, plan to sell them for no more than the cover price plus tax. Because you can buy books from publishers at a trade discount when you buy in quantity, you will still make money (often 50 percent of the cover price).

If you want to sell tapes, be sure you work with a professional who can get good quality audiotapes, help you edit them, and help you find someone who can duplicate them in bulk. This person also should help you design and produce the "J" cards that slip into the plastic case and describe the tape. If you want to produce videotapes, working with a professional is something you must do to be sure you are creating a quality tape that you will be proud to sell. In the case of audiotapes or video-tapes that you produce yourself, you can set the price at what-ever you want it to be; just be careful not to set it so high that people are reluctant to purchase it.

Depending on your locality, you may have to charge a sales tax. To collect that tax, you need a resale license. In this case, you will not pay tax when you purchase materials for resale, but you will charge tax to the end users and then, on the schedule set by your taxing authority, you will fill out a form and submit those tax monies. A resale license is not normally difficult to get. You can find out the local regulations by talking with your accountant or looking under "Taxes" in the government section of your phone book.

When the Seminar Is Over

As your seminar is coming toward its conclusion, let the students know that you are available to them. You might offer to answer questions for five minutes over the phone for free or just let them know where they can reach you.

After you have told them this, end your seminar on a strong note with a great success story or an exciting call to action. This is a much stronger ending than just telling them where to reach you and having them walk out the door. Students are more likely to remember the seminar as exciting if they leave on a high note than if the event just ends on a sales pitch.

At this time, also be sure that you have the necessary information to get back to any students for whom you promised to answer questions that you couldn't answer during the seminar. Be sure you have all the paperwork you need, especially if you have to turn in a roster to the sponsoring organization in order to be paid. Be sure you collect the evaluation sheets. Consider placing a box near the exit so students can drop the forms in as they leave in case students are reluctant to give them to you personally.

Finally, after you get back to the office, take a few moments and write thank-you notes to anyone who was especially helpful to you in making the seminar possible. You may want to work with these people again in the future and everyone loves to be appreciated.

SELF-SURVEY: WORKSHEET FOR EVALUATING CUSTOMER/CLIENT EDUCATION SEMINAR OPTIONS

What will the topic of my seminar/workshop be? _____

_____

My title will be: _____

Places were I could teach it: _____

_____

_____

Date called for catalog: _____

Elements I want to be sure to include in my course outline:

_____

_____

_____

Elements I want to include with my proposal:

☐ Cover letter

☐ Resume

☐ Outline

List of needed equipment: _____

_____

_____

Letters of recommendation: _____

Date proposal sent: _____

Date scheduled to teach seminar/workshop: _____

Results: _____

_____

_____

_____

8

Profiting On-Line with Computers

PROMOTING YOUR BUSINESS ON-LINE

By now, you have probably heard hundreds of times that big profits can be made on-line if you are just clever enough to do it. There is some truth to that, but like anything else, there is a learning curve to deal with, especially if you are not already comfortable with the virtual world.

There can also be a hefty price tag for some of the options you are considering. A recent article in *PC World Magazine* states that the annual fee for having an electronic storefront on CompuServe starts at $10,000 per year!

However, there are ways that you can promote yourself and your business on-line for little or no money. This chapter provides an overview of the process. If you decide to pursue this opportunity, be sure to read *Computerizing Your Business,* which is another book in the Prentice Hall *Run Your Own Business* series.

Ways You Can Benefit

When faced with the need to learn a new skill, it is only normal to ask, "What's in it for me?" Learning how to use your computer to promote your business is no different. So here are some of the ways you can profit. The benefits you achieve will only be limited by how much time you devote to it and how much you are willing to learn.

- E-mail. This term means "electronic mail." E-mail enables you to send communications instantly to any other person or business that has an e-mail address anywhere in the world. According to Mike Albrecht in *Computerizing Your Business,* e-mail is the most used Internet resource and is the primary reason that most Internet users are on the Net. He adds that 37 percent of all mail delivered in the United States in April 1994 was sent electronically and the figure is continuing to rise. Some companies are now using e-mail to place orders to ensure their order gets through correctly and immediately.

- Networking. While networking can be done by individual correspondence, networking is much more than merely correspondence. Using your computer, you can tap into discussions with people who share similar interests. Depending on where you find these discussions, they may be called conferences, forums, boards, special interest groups, or newsgroups. The beauty of these places is that you can usually "lurk" and just read what other people are saying or leave messages either responding to other people's concerns or expressing concerns of your own. This way you can both learn what concerns are important to others in your field and get support from your peers who may be anywhere in the world.

- Soft-sell. When you are on-line in different forums, boards, etc., you can promote yourself by demonstrating your expertise. You can do this by answering other people's questions or offering advice. If you do this, don't say, "I have that information and I use it to help my clients." The aim is to show you at your best so that people will seek you out. It is considered rude and tacky to blatantly push your products or services. Remember that when you are writing in these forum-type places, your message is being read by many more people than you addressed it to. It may also be read by a *sysop* (system operator who is an expert on how to utilize the forum and its materials) who may have the ability to remove it from the forum if he or she determines that the material is too obviously self-promotional.

■ Research. Using the on-line services like CompuServe and America On-Line or going on the Internet by using a browser to explore the World Wide Web, you can tap into current publications, extensive libraries, governmental data banks, and almost anything else you can think of. You can get the latest research or do a review of literature on a particular topic from a historical perspective. Abigail Albrecht, who does on-line research for her clients, says that people need to remember that the information they want can often be found for "free," although free is a relative term. On one hand, you will not have to pay the newsstand price to read an article. On the other hand, you may have to pay connect time charges of several dollars an hour (which can add up quickly) if you are going through a commercial service like CompuServe or America On-Line. There may also be download charges for some information. She adds that for people who are not accustomed to doing research on-line, "It really is a test of endurance to try to get everything you need from the Web without clicking on random links."

Whatever you want to know, you can probably find it by using your computer to surf the Web. If you are not comfortable with the many ways to explore the Web, take a class through a computer store or local college to help you get familiar with the different ways you can benefit. If time is an issue, hire someone who has the experience and skills to do a search for you quickly. Also, watch for articles and workshops offered through professional publications and meetings that will help you better access the information that is important to you.

UNDERSTANDING THE ETIQUETTE CALLED NETIQUETTE

As with any social interaction, communication on-line carries with it its own set of accepted rules that have become recognized as good manners. Violating them can result in being chided (either in a forum, list, or private mail) to disciplinary action by the on-line service or Web interface service that you are using. There are two layers of etiquette to consider when you are thinking about using electronic communication to promote your business. The first is *general netiquette,* basic manners, if you will. Second, there is *business netiquette,* the special nuances you need to be aware of if you want to project the best possible image and avoid errors that can negatively impact your efforts.

Certainly, the best set of user guidelines and netiquette has been developed by Arlene Rinaldi. In her Web page (http://vs6000.adm.fau.edu/rinaldi/arlene.html), she gives others permission to reprint her guidelines, so with thanks to her, here they are:

- Keep paragraphs and messages short and to the point.

- Focus on one subject per message and always include a pertinent subject title for the message; that way the user can locate the message quickly.

- Don't use the academic networks for commercial or proprietary work.

- Include your signature at the bottom of e-mail messages. Your signature footer should include your name, position, affiliation, and on-line address(es) and should not exceed four lines. Optional information could include your home address and phone number.

- Capitalize words only to highlight an important point or to distinguish a title or heading. *Asterisks* surrounding a word also can be used to make a stronger point. Capitalizing whole words that are not titles is generally termed as SHOUTING!

- Limit line length and avoid control characters.

- Follow chain of command procedures for corresponding with superiors. For example, don't send a complaint via e-mail directly to the "top" just because you can.

- Be professional and careful about what you say about others. E-mail is easily forwarded.

- Cite all quotes, references, and sources and respect copyright and license agreements.

- It is considered extremely rude to forward personal e-mail to mailing lists or Usenet without the original author's permission.

- Be careful when using sarcasm and humor. Without face-to-face communications your joke may be viewed as criticism.

- Acronyms can be used to abbreviate when possible; however messages that are filled with acronyms can be confusing and annoying to the reader.

Examples of acronyms are as follows:

IMHO = in my humble/honest opinion

FYI = for your information

BTW = by the way

Flame = antagonistic criticism

:-) = happy face for humor

Copyright by Arlene Rinaldi, used by permission.

Business Netiquette

The rules above are considered basic good manners for your electronic communications. In addition, there are certain guidelines you will be expected to adhere to in promoting your business on-line.

The first major rule is that you do not go around *spamming* (sending an overwhelming volume of messages to one person or sending an unsolicited message to many people) everyone you can reach with unsolicited advertising. Some people promote this as a way of generating business, but it is considered the height of bad manners in the virtual world. (If you'd like to see a humorous and somewhat irreverent Web page on spamming, go to http://sp1.berkeley.edu/findthespam.html.)

Business netiquette is more subtle and elegant. When done properly, it also has the advantage of building an image of you and your business as leading experts in your field. As you read in Chapters 4 to 7, building a strong, positive public image can lead to opportunities you could never have imagined. Your electronic image will contribute to that overall impact.

The rules you need to remember when you are promoting your business on-line are on pages 123-124. Photocopy these pages and post them next to your computer to help you when a confusing situation arises.

Al Bredenberg, author of *The Small Business Guide to Internet Marketing*, gives three additional tips to ensure you get the most from your marketing efforts on-line:

1. Use the correct spelling, punctuation, and grammar. He admits to being surprised at how much poorly written copy he sees on the Internet. Bredenberg advises people to carefully project a professional image by paying attention to how they write.

2. He advises you include a clear call to action in your message for the reader. What do you want the reader to do? Ask for more information? Request a proposal? Ask for a price quote? You need to let the readers know what you expect them to do and be sure you make it easy for them to respond to you through your e-mail link. This also means you should check your e-mail and/or forum postings at least once, preferably twice, a day so that you can respond to inquiries promptly.

3. Finally, Bredenberg suggests you let your regular customers and the public know about your Web page and e-mail address. Put the addresses on your stationery, ads, brochures, packaging, etc. The addresses can serve to both create new business relationships and strengthen the ones you currently have.

CREATING YOUR OWN WEB PAGE

You have probably already been wondering if having a Web page would help promote your business. Many people are finding that these pages are an ongoing source of new customers and revenue. However, a badly done Web page is worse than not having one at all. So what do you need to know so that your page is a success?

Do Not	Do
1. Do not blatantly advertise or solicit business.	**1.** Do create an image as an expert in your field/industry.
2. Do not send unsolicited advertisements or promotional materials.	**2.** Do have materials available to e-mail or snail-mail anyone who contacts you as a result of reading something you wrote on-line.
3. Do not be heavy-handed and/or insulting when responding to on-line messages you disagree with. It can annoy the people administering the system and result in your being banned from the forum. More important, it gives you a highly negative image in the minds of others in the forum—just the people you were hoping to impress positively.	**3.** Do make your expertise known by offering helpful information in forum messages on on-line services to which you subscribe. See note 7 if you do not know how to find those forums.
4. Do not expect instant results.	**4.** Do expect on-line marketing to be an ongoing effort that will normally have an increasing level of success (many marketing experts will tell you that people need to hear/see your name approximately seven times before they will feel comfortable contacting you).
5. Do not play games. Don't leave messages saying that you "wish you could help, but ... " Remember, forums are set up to share information, not to make life difficult for people who are looking for clients/customers.	**5.** Do give helpful information when you respond to other people's questions. You don't have to give away everything you know, but sharing a piece of useful information establishes you as an expert (and a nice person to do business with).

Do Not	Do
6. Do not make every answer you give others in a forum situation a brazen advertisement that mentions your services/products and fees/costs.	**6.** Do develop a signature footer for your e-mail that includes your name, position, affiliation, and e-mail address. This gives any reader (even lurkers) a way of contacting you personally for more information. An example of a signature footer follows: Josephine Jones, President Your Supplier, Inc. Home Town, USA E-mail: XXXXXX.XXX
7. Do not assume that if writing something on-line sounds good to you, and does not violate any of the rules above, it is acceptable. The rules of social niceties and legal responsibility (i.e., libel) still hold.	**7.** Do get in touch with the sysop or membership function of each on-line service or Usenet and ask him or her for any specific rules they have for people who promote their businesses through that service and the forums that cover your areas of interest.

According to Robert Moskowitz's article in *MicroTimes*, before beginning a Web page, consider what you want it to do for you, who your target readers are, and what they expect to find there. He advises that you keep it simple. Most Web users prefer it that way because it allows them to download your page more quickly.

Also, you need to be aware that a Web page is not a static thing. You will need to update it at least several times a year. If you set it up so that you get a complete list of the e-mail addresses of everyone who connects with it, you will need to service it regularly in order to harvest those names and send them promotional materials.

You will want to make your page interesting by including several elements including the following:

- Headings. Use different heading levels to set off the separate parts of your document and help readers find the parts that interest them quickly. Be careful not to make them so large that they disrupt the design of your page.

- Text. Have written text material prepared that describes your business and what you have to offer readers. Be sure you give people ways to contact you on-line and by telephone or mail.

- Lists. Use lists to set apart brief bits of information in a visually interesting way.

- Links. Use links to connect the readers of your Web page to other sites on the Internet and to help the readers of those pages to find you. You can connect with other pages involved in similar businesses, professional organizations, or just about anyone you can think of.

  Ask for permission from the owner of the other Web page before you connect to it and don't forget to ask if he or she will link his or her page to yours. Be sure to access all the pages you want to link to. The reason to do that is to make sure that the places people might link to from your page are acceptable to you. It certainly will not do your business any good if people start with your page and end up at a page that is vulgar or pornographic.

- Images. Add excitement to your page and enable people to see anything from your business logo to the merchandise you offer by using graphic images. Just remember that too many images or images that are too large will take a great deal of time for most people to download, which can make them irritated with you before they even read your information.

When custom bridal headwear designer Lisa Steinberg was designing her Web page, she took the complaints she had heard from other Web users about the length of time it can take to download images seriously. She wanted her page to be easy to read and have a lot of text links to other pages.

This philosophy has worked out well for Steinberg; she currently gets about fifty hits a day and is gratified with the inquiries she gets from brides seeking affordable, custom head-wear for their weddings. Her Web page can be found at http://user.aol.com/lsbridal/private/lsbridal.htm.

Getting Started

The actual work of creating your Web page can be done in a day or two. There are programs available to assist you and you can get them at any major computer software store. Some on-line services also may be willing to assist you or supply you with the software you need.

If you want to do it yourself, consider taking an extension course at a local college or from other adult learning programs for special classes to help you write your page. You could also hire someone who specializes in creating Web pages (they exist!) to help you. Such people can be found through computer magazines, personal referrals from people whose pages you admire, and referrals from people who work at your local computer store. Another great resource you should access if you want to do your Web page yourself is at Indiana University. It includes HTML tutorials, references, and technical documentation. It can be reached on-line at http://www-slis.lib.indiana.edu/Internet/programmer-page.html.

The costs associated with your Web page will normally be minimal. To have a simple page through a vendor who has an Internet-connected computer should cost you less than fifty dollars per month. Costs through the major on-line services may be higher.

Remember that there are several levels of benefit for you if you go on-line with a Web page. It can bring in new clients, make your name better known to people who are interested in your industry, and just help you meet other people who share your interests.

Eppie Archuleta hardly fits the typical "image" of Web page owner. In her mid-70s, Archuleta is a gifted textile artist who has been profiled in *National Geographic*. Her work also has been shown in the Smithsonian. Her artworks bring in thousands of dollars each. She maintains her business, which includes her art and a woolen mill that produces high-quality yarn from local wool, all in a small community in Colorado.

At the suggestion of Noel Dunne of the ecumenical Christian Community Services (a group working on pilot projects to enable local people to economically revitalize the area), Archuleta went on-line with the assistance of a VISTA volunteer who did the programming. Her page offers information about herself, her wool, and the Capulin Mill, images of her weavings, and an order form for people who want to purchase her marvelous yarns. (If you want to see her page, it is at http://www.rmii.com/~ccs/index.html.)

Archuleta has had thousands of "hits" of people visiting her page. She has enjoyed some orders for her yarn and has made some new contacts with people who share her passion for weaving.

Other people who have businesses that are of more general interest often have more visitors and resulting contacts. The success of your page will be determined by how many people are interested in your topic and how many links you establish with similar pages that help bring people into your page.

SPECIAL RESOURCES AVAILABLE ON-LINE

As you gain familiarity with the on-line services you use and the Internet, you will discover myriad resources you can tap into to answer nearly any question you have.

A good place to start is with on-line services. Check their menus for topics such as business or profession. These topics may lead you to forums and bulletin boards that will help you with everything from marketing to ethics. Then look for a command that says "keyword" or "Go to" and type in a word or two that are specific to your business or the topic you are trying to get more information about. If you are new at this and find something similar but not exactly what you are looking for, it is acceptable to post a message asking for referrals to other areas you will want to explore.

Check with your professional organizations to see if they have any private forums and/or chat rooms on a service. You won't find these just by looking around, you have to be "toggled in" (put on the list of those who have access to the area) before they will show up on your computer screen. These private areas can be a marvelous source of networking, support, and up-to-the-minute information. Some organizations also may have a Web page. If your organization does, be sure to access it. You may find new membership benefits you didn't even realize were available to you!

Once you have mastered the use of on-line services, try looking around the Internet for more information. Once you are on, you can go to a search mode using a browser like Mosiac or Netscape that are available by downloading from the Internet. Alternatively, you can purchase these browsers for a modest price at most computer software stores. If you might spend a lot of time accessing information on the Internet, you will want to open an account with a local Internet access provider. This will allow you to have unlimited access to the Internet for a nominal monthly fee (often under $25). Your local computer store can tell you which ones in your area offer good quality service.

If you just want to start looking around, here are several sites you can browse:

- The Consortium for Global Commerce focuses on facilitating international trade, investment, and strategic cooperation initiatives by utilizing the synergy created when people and organizations join together to achieve a common goal. Through this Web page, you can access the Global Network of Chambers of Commerce, the Global Business Opportunities Exchange, the Merchants & Commercial Service Providers, and other like-minded organizations. The Web address is http://www.usa1.com/~ibnet/cgchp.html.

- EINet Galaxy's Business and Commerce Directory has a list of electronic, commerce-related Web sites. Be sure to look under the "Business and Commerce" topic for areas of interest including "Business General Resources," "Electronic Commerce," and "Marketing and Sales." You will also enjoy going to the "Reference and Interdisciplinary Information" topic and checking out the "Internet and Networking" area. The Web page address is http://lmc.einet.net/.

■ Yahoo Business Directories is a highly current catalog of businesses on the Web. Topics you can access here include "Business Directory," "Electronic Commerce," "Marketing," "Small Business Information," and "Conventions and Conferences." The Web address is http://www.yahoo.com/business.

Finally, for a little fun and a business-oriented comic, try The Dilbert Zone at http://www.unitedmedia.com/comics/dilbert/.

SELF-SURVEY: WORKSHEET FOR CREATING AN ACTION PLAN TO PROMOTE YOUR BUSINESS ON-LINE

Using On-Line Forums

On-line services I belong to: _____

_____

Forums on those services relating to my business: _____

_____

Date last visited: _____

Comments I made/Questions I answered for others: _____

_____

Response I received from others on forum: _____

_____

Creating My Web Page:

Goal I hope to achieve through this page: _____

_____

Value I can offer through my page: _____

_____

Response I hope to receive from my readers: _____

_____

How I plan to write my page (for example, self, attend class, hire someone): _____

Other pages I can link to mine: _____

How I will deal with responses: (Tip: Any materials you plan to have available to send to those who respond to your page should be ready before your page goes on-line.) _____

_____

9

Customer Service: The Under-Recognized Key to Building Your Business

If someone asked you who the most important person in your business is, what would you answer? Yourself? A key employee? A supplier who makes sure you have the products you need? All these answers are wrong. The most important person to your business is your customer or client. Without people to buy your goods or services, you have a hobby—not a business.

In this chapter, we will cover many key areas you need to pay attention to if you want to succeed. All of these areas focus on making your business more attractive to the customers you have and to the customers you would like to have.

Before we get down to the nuts and bolts, remember that you should find ways that are uniquely yours to let your customers know they are appreciated, whether it is keeping a fresh pot of coffee by the reception desk or something more creative.

Remember Dave Lakhani from Chapter 3? He is the computer store owner who puts on a yearly computer swap meet that has been a valuable tool to bring in new customers. He's always thinking of new ways to serve his customers—even on his honeymoon! Lakhani says, "I never miss an opportunity to send a card. I sent all my best customers postcards from my honeymoon in Grand Cayman, thanking them for making my honeymoon possible and offering them 15 percent off any purchase they made within a week of receiving the postcard. Those postcards were good for $9,000 in sales in one week."

While you are starting to think of the ways you can improve your customer service, let's start with the basics.

MAKING YOUR BUSINESS APPEAR WELCOMING

The way your business looks will have a lasting impact on your potential customers. You have undoubtedly experienced this yourself.

For example, imagine two retail establishments. One has its aisles cluttered with boxes of merchandise and the shelves and racks are disorganized and difficult to search through. The other has wide, clear aisles and the merchandise is neatly stacked and displayed with clear signs to help you. Which one will you want to shop in?

If you have a business where you provide a professional service rather than merchandise, you probably have a waiting area. Is it a no-man's-land of stained furniture, ancient magazines, and the occasional used coffee cup? Or is it an inviting atmosphere presenting a professional image with comfortable furniture, current magazines, product brochures or videos about your industry being shown on a television, and maybe a water cooler or pot of fresh coffee?

The image that customers see when they first encounter your place of business will influence your relationship with them. Do they get the impression that you are organized or chaotic? Does your decorating scheme tend to intimidate them, horrify them, or make them comfortable? If you didn't know how skilled and competent you are, would you want to do business with someone who's place of business looked like yours?

See Through Your Customers' Eyes

Take a few minutes to see your workplace as others see it. Start by going outside. Then ask yourself these questions:

- Is my sign easy to spot and read? Can it be seen by people driving by? Is it clearly lit at night?
- Is there adequate parking? Can my customers find it easily?
- Are the sidewalks and parking areas free of litter and debris?
- Is the landscaping tidy and attractive?
- Is my front door paint in good condition and are the windows clean?
- Is there adequate light for customers coming after dark?

Then move inside and ask yourself:

- Is the entry/reception area welcoming?
- If you share the building, are there clear directions on a directory board or a receptionist to direct customers to you?
- If there is a directory board, are your name and your company name spelled correctly?
- If your business is not retail, can customers tell what you do by looking around? Are there displays of your professional licenses, diplomas, projects, awards, or copies of articles about you and your business prominently exhibited?
- If your business is retail, is merchandise displayed in an attractive and inviting way? Do your displays give customers new ideas about innovative ways to use the products they came to buy as well as inspire them to purchase additional products to help them achieve their lifestyle goals?

Remember All the Senses

While there is no mistaking the importance of creating a positive visual effect for customers and clients in your business, it is also important to pay attention to the senses of hearing and smell.

You may have noticed that many businesses (especially dentists' offices!) use background music. That music can help both to relax people and to keep voices from carrying between rooms or through thin walls. Some retail establishments have even experimented with background music that has subliminal messages to discourage shoplifting. If you think background music might be useful in your business, first consider the type of music you want to use. Rock, heavy-metal, or rap music may suit you or your employees, but will it offend your customers? You might want to play a radio station or personal CDs. You need to get a license (for a nominal fee) to protect yourself from lawsuits if you use any copyrighted music. Call ASCAP's licensing department at 212-631-6403 for information.

You also must deal with the issue of smell. If you doubt that it is important, ask your friendly neighborhood real estate agent why so many agents warm a loaf of bread in the oven or place a dab of vanilla extract on light bulbs when they are showing a home to prospective buyers. If you use medical supplies, office products, or other chemicals that give off an odor, you are probably so accustomed to the smell that you don't notice it any more, but you can bet that your customers do. If you just have a slight odor to overcome, one or two open bowls of potpourri may make the office more fragrant. If you need more help, consider purchasing air fresheners available at grocery and drug stores to make the air quality in your business more welcoming.

EMPLOYEES—YOUR GOODWILL AMBASSADORS

Even if you have the most beautiful business site in the world, you will not have the success you crave if your employees are not focused on customer satisfaction.

Have you ever walked away from a purchase because the salesclerk was on the phone with a friend and found that more interesting than helping you? Many people do.

Have you ever decided not to do business with a professional because of the rude way his or her employees treated you or because you heard them gossiping about other clients and decided you didn't want your personal business broadcast that way?

You would be amazed at how important your employees' attitudes are to your business success. In her book, *Fabled Service*, Betsy Sanders explains why companies lose customers. She says that 1 percent die, 3 percent move away, and another 5 percent are influenced by their friends. All the dollars spent on advertising and other efforts only result in 9 percent being lured away by the competition.

Now come the interesting numbers: Fourteen percent of customers no longer use a product because they are dissatisfied with it. This is something you may be able to correct. Amazingly, a full 68 percent stop doing business with a company because they feel turned away by an attitude of indifference on the part of a company employee. This is certainly something that you can correct.

The first step in having your employees be goodwill ambassadors for your business is to hire the right employees. It may sound simple, but it can be very easy to overlook the potential employee whose experience in your area is not good in favor of someone who is more seasoned. However, if seasoned employees have poor "people" skills, their superior experience will be useless because they will annoy customers. On the other hand, an employee who has great people skills will often be eager to be taught the business skills needed to be successful.

Once you have hired the right people, you need to train them properly so they will know what you expect from them. Do they know how you expect them to greet customers or clients? Have you reviewed the techniques you expect them to use on the telephone? Do they know what areas you are willing to give them some leeway on so they can handle customer concerns immediately? What else should they know to be best able to serve your business?

Plan to spend some time with your employees going over your business philosophy and how you expect them to act in common circumstances. Role playing exercises can be very helpful training tools. Have one employee play the part of the customer in different circumstances. One could be an ordinary sale, another could be a customer who is in a hurry, another could be a customer who is dissatisfied for some reason. Then have an employee play the part of "your employee." Observe the exercise and see if you can point out better ways to handle the situation. Be sure to praise your employees when they do well.

Be sure to listen to your employees when you are doing these training sessions and when they are talking about the customers. It can be valuable to ask them, "What areas do our customers seem to feel we could handle better?" and "What do you think we could do to serve our clients better?" The employees who are dealing with the customers personally will often have valuable input for you. Consider having some sort of award or recognition for employees who give you feedback you can use.

Finally, it is important that you give your employees a sense that they are contributing to the success of the business and that your business is interested in their personal success. Growth is a natural phenomenon and people will be happier and more willing to invest their energy in your business if they feel that they are learning and growing at the same time. Even the smallest business can have opportunities for the employees to learn new skills in their work. You also might consider ways your business can support employees' learning goals by helping them attend college courses or seminars that will help them update their current skills and learn new skills that are related to your business.

Be Sure Your Employees Know What You Do

This may sound like a no-brainer, but you need to be sure your employees do know exactly what you do and what your business supplies. Take some time today and ask your employees what they tell their friends and family about their employer. You may be surprised.

In her book, *Jesus CEO*, Laurie Beth Jones tells of a time when she was giving a series of seminars at an osteopathic hospital in Texas. One of the first things she discovered there was that 75 percent of the hospital staff did not know what the term "osteopathic" meant! This fine facility had spent nearly half a million dollars educating the public about its mission, but the staff who worked there were still in the dark.

Jones was able to give the seminar attendees a knowledge of what "osteopathic" meant beyond the dictionary definition. She also imparted an excitement about the mission of the hospital that had them asking for fliers to pass out to their friends.

Just think of the number of strangers, family members, and friends these people then told about what they had learned! Think of the way they were able to help potential patients understand the hospital's purpose for the rest of their employment. What can you teach your employees so that they will be able to explain your business to the people they meet?

PROFITABLE CUSTOMER RECOURSE POLICIES

"Customer Satisfaction" and "Customer Service" are two phrases that are heard everywhere in business these days. If you go to any bookstore, you will see many titles on this subject, and several that you see will be considered to be best-sellers. Most of the books discuss overall theories or deal with huge corporations. But what can you do to ensure customer satisfaction?

No matter how careful you are in your business, there will be times when your customer or client is dissatisfied with your goods or services. How you handle this situation will determine whether you keep or lose this person's business—or even if you end up in court! More than that, a dissatisfied person will tell his or her friends and family about the bad experience. And then those people will tell others.

You will never know how much each dissatisfied customer costs you. On the other hand, if you can offer that customer a way of gaining satisfaction from the problem, you have strengthened the bond that brings him or her back—and they are likely to share the good news of your extra effort with friends and family.

To paraphrase an old saying that has been posted in many businesses over the years, there are two rules for customer service:

1. The customer is always right.
2. If the customer is wrong, refer to rule #1.

When Troubles Arise

The key to keeping customers satisfied is what you do to help them when something goes wrong. To be sure you are ready when something (inevitably) will go wrong, you need to plan how you will handle warranties/guarantees up front and merchandise returns or customer dissatisfaction when they occur.

You've probably already had customers ask for guarantees or warranties on your products or services. As you know, a *warranty* is the written explanation of the manufacturer's promise to "stand behind" a product if it proves to be defective or performs poorly. The warranty should clearly state how long it is good for and what exactly is covered. As a businessperson, you must be sure you understand the manufacturers' warranties for the items you sell so that you can help your customers if they need to make a claim against a warranty.

A *guarantee*, on the other hand, is your promise that you or your business are responsible for the performance of the goods or services you have sold. The way you stand behind your guarantee tells your customers how committed you are to their satisfaction.

Sometimes, you can be put in an awkward position because of warranties and guarantees given by manufacturers that they fail to stand behind. Then you are put in the difficult position of having to decide whether to protect your short-term finances by standing with the manufacturer or protecting your business relationships by standing with your customer.

Don McCulley knows firsthand how that goes. He is a sales agent for hardware and building materials producers that do not have their own sales staff. At one point, he took on a new line of lighting that used motion sensors to turn on the lamps. He approached a retailer who was interested in the product, but had some reservations.

The retailer requested a money-back guarantee if he was unable to sell the lights and McCulley contacted the manufacturer and got the guarantee in writing. A few months after the retailer stocked the merchandise, he and McCulley discovered that the manufacturer was undermining the retail market for the device by offering it through tool magazines at below the price the retailer would have to charge. Understandably, the retailer wanted to return the unsold merchandise for a refund.

Because McCulley had gotten a written guarantee, he did not anticipate any problems. However, the manufacturer came up with the astounding offer to take back the merchandise, but *not* refund the money!

So McCulley was in a very tough position. If he backed the manufacturer, he would destroy his relationship with the retailer. If he backed the retailer, it would mean a significant dent in his own finances.

McCulley is a man of honor, so he kept the commitment to the retailer. He returned the man's money and took back the lamps. He also severed his relationship with the manufacturer. To this day, he has an excellent relationship with the retailer and feels good about the choice he made.

If Your Business Is Retail

When you have a retail business, one of the areas where customer satisfaction problems are often caused is in handling returned merchandise. If you have not developed a clear policy to handle returned merchandise, start doing it right now.

Check with business associations and governmental agencies to be sure there are not local laws that determine what your merchandise return policy should be. If you are not constrained by law, confer with other merchants in your community to see what their return policies are, as customers tend to expect similar policies in the same geographical area.

Some of the policies you might consider include:

- All sales final—No returns
- Returns only within thirty days and must have receipt

- Returns only for defective merchandise
- Returns accepted any time for any reason

Does that last policy sound a little foolhardy? It's not! You will sometimes hear stories of how a well-known merchant accepted returned merchandise it hadn't ever sold at that store and made a customer for life. No one is suggesting that you should accept every item a customer tries to return, but you should try to create a policy that you can live with and that will make your customers feel they are dealing with someone who cares about their satisfaction.

Part of creating a customer-friendly merchandise return policy is training your staff to handle these situations courteously. Some people who are making returns or expressing other complaints may not behave as well as they might. They usually are upset about the problem and they may not be very comfortable dealing with it. Some people can come across as nervous, angry, or even rude. Your employees need to recognize that these situations should not be treated as personal attacks on them, but instead should be treated as opportunities to solve a problem. When your employees can help the customers resolve their problems, everyone will feel better and your business will likely have strengthened its relationship with that person.

If Your Business Is Service

Service businesses can include anything from accounting to dentistry to plumbing to writing. If you have this kind of business, then people are counting on you to do something for them that they cannot do themselves.

The most important factor to customers is that they can trust you. This trust covers a lot of territory. They need to trust you to be:

- Honest and ethical
- Competent to do your work
- Able to maintain confidentiality
- Able to give accurate quotes of expenses

- Able to give accurate estimates of time involved
- Pleasant to deal with no matter how the rest of your day has gone
- Able to be reached in an emergency

Even if you are all of these things, there may come a day when a client feels dissatisfied. Again, you need to remember that the customer is expressing feelings and not really attacking you (although as the service provider you may feel more like a target than a retail employee would).

You also need to keep in mind that any time a client comes to you with a complaint, they are actually giving you an opportunity to make your business better. Think about the ways you could use the following complaints to improve your business:

Complaint: The home renovations you completed do not look the way the client thought they should.

Business lesson: Perhaps your contracts with clients should spell out the exact materials, colors, and so on better than they do now.

Complaint: Your patient broke a tooth on Saturday morning and couldn't reach you for emergency repairs because you were out of town.

Business lesson: Maybe you should team up with another dentist or two and develop an after-hours answering service so all of you can cover for one another as needed.

Complaint: The person who bought an insurance policy from you is upset because something she thought was covered was denied by the insurance company.

Business lesson: Could you do a better job of explaining benefits and coverages to your clients? Is there other supporting documentation you can give them with their policies to help the clients understand them? If there is a reasonable question about the coverage, can you advocate for your customer with the company and possibly get them some benefits?

On a separate sheet of paper, write down the one or two complaints you have heard the most. Now brainstorm a list of potential ways you can do a better job so that these complaints will not happen again in the future.

If you are tempted to write off the complainers as not being important to your business, you need to know some more figures from Betsy Sander's book. She writes that the average customer or client who has a complaint will tell nine to ten people about their dissatisfaction. A full 13 percent will tell more than twenty people each! So if you want to stay in business and prosper, it is just good common sense to keep your customers and clients satisfied.

Don't Wait for Complaints

Since it is inevitable that you will get some complaints and/or returned merchandise from time to time, the trick is to reduce the number of incidences and handle them quickly. Ideally, you will discover potential problems and correct them while they are still small irritations and before they become full-fledged problems.

One way to do that is to have customer satisfaction forms. They could be on a countertop, on the back of a bill (like at a restaurant), enclosed with a mailing, etc. You have undoubtedly already seen similar forms at some businesses, like hotels where they are frequently in the room when you arrive.

Your form should be brief and have some space to allow for personal comments. If you have the forms available at your place of business, it is a good idea to ask the customers to fill in the date of their visit and the name of the employee who helped them (this will allow you to catch your employees doing a wonderful job as well as correct any customer-service problems). You might ask the customers a few yes-or-no questions or ask them to rate certain aspects of your business on a scale of one to five. A customer comment card at a restaurant might include the information shown in the sample on page 143.

Whatever your business is, you can probably make a brief list of questions that will help you learn what your customers think about the service you offer. Do not try to cover everything in one customer survey. If the survey has too many questions, no one will bother to fill it out.

Please rate your visit to our restaurant on a scale of 1 to 5, with 5 being excellent and 1 being unacceptable.

	(5)	(4)	(3)	(2)	(1)
Was your order prepared properly?	☐	☐	☐	☐	☐
Was your food served hot?	☐	☐	☐	☐	☐
Was your food served promptly?	☐	☐	☐	☐	☐
Was the presentation attractive?	☐	☐	☐	☐	☐
Was the restaurant clean?	☐	☐	☐	☐	☐
Was your server helpful?	☐	☐	☐	☐	☐

Other comments: _____

_____

_____

_____

Date of visit: _____

Server: _____

Two more thoughts on using customer satisfaction cards:

1. Don't make your customers go out and find an envelope and stamp to return the survey—or you'll never see it again. Consider either enclosing the survey with a bill to them (and they can return it with their payment) or printing it on a postage-paid postcard they can just drop into a mailbox.
2. If you want a lot of feedback quickly, offer a prize for the card that is drawn out of all the cards returned by a certain date. It can be something relatively small like lunch for two at a local restaurant or a complimentary service from you.

In conclusion, remember the figures given earlier in the chapter about why businesses lose customers. The most important one to remember is that 68 percent of customers who are lost stop doing business with you because they feel an attitude of indifference on the part of your company or your employee. While some loss of customers is probably inevitable, imagine what your profits would be if you could suddenly regain that 68 percent of the customers you have lost over the years!

Now, make a commitment to providing better service to the customers you have and you will be amazed at how quickly and well it pays off.

Self-Survey: Worksheet for Achieving Superior Customer Service

Walk into your business, pretending to be a customer.

What impresses you favorably? _____

_____

What needs work? _____

_____

What can you do today to start improving the things that need work? _____

_____

How do your employees relate to customers? _____

_____

Which employees need more training? _____
How I plan to accomplish that training: _____

_____

What is my current customer recourse policy? _____

_____

What can I do to make it more attractive for my customers?

_____

Who should I talk to about regulations or common local practices on customer recourse policies? _____
What training will my employees need on this new policy?

_____

Would a customer satisfaction survey help me serve my customers? If so, how should I implement it (for example, supply postage-paid postcard, send with bills, place cards on counter)? _____

10

Integrating Several Promotional Concepts

As you have read through this book, you have undoubtedly come up with some promotional ideas you would like to implement. Now the challenge is to do that in a way that gives you the maximum possible benefit for your work.

A word that really applies here is *synergy.* In simple terms, synergy is when two or more elements join together and the resulting value is more than the value of the elements separately.

An example of synergy could be a restaurant owner who hires two cooks. If both her cooks are excellent bread bakers, but neither is good at making main dishes, she has two good employees but not much of a menu—and no synergy. On the other hand, if one employee is good at baking breads and the other makes marvelous main dishes, the meals at this restaurant will be in great demand. These two employees are working togeth-er with synergy to make the restaurant more successful.

CREATING SYNERGY BY COMBINING PROMOTIONAL EFFORTS

To create synergy in your promotional efforts, start by thinking of the different types of activities you have been learning about in this book:

- Working with other businesses
- Working with charities and non-profits
- Sponsoring events to get attention
- Getting noticed by the media
- Writing for publication
- Giving speeches
- Putting on seminars
- Marketing on-line
- Improving customer service

Now start thinking about ways you can combine two or more of these activities. Obviously, getting noticed by the media is some-thing you should pursue with nearly every promotional effort you make. In some cases, like when working with charities, the charities may take care of this angle for you. With small groups, you may choose to offer to handle it yourself just to be sure the media are contacted in time to cover the story.

Ways to Make It Work

Below are five potential situations to help you imagine how you could combine your promotional efforts. For each situation men-tioned, there are two ways the businessperson might consider combining two or more elements from this book synergistically to achieve the goal. You will notice that the first option in each case will require a substantial commitment in terms of time. The second option is created for people who want a free or low-cost promotion, but have very limited time available for this purpose.

Situation: You have a vegetarian restaurant and want to promote healthy eating.

Option 1: Offer a seminar. You might contact the local Heart Association or other health-related group and ask for co-sponsorship, a free room to hold the seminar in, or help in publicizing your seminar through the organization's newsletter.

Write a press release about the seminar for newspapers and a PSA (public service announcement) for local radio stations. Also, consider working together with another complementary business, such as a health club, to offer a more wide-ranging health program.

Option 2: Enter a team of employees in a charity-sponsored cook-off event. Send press releases announcing your participation to local media before the event (and again after the event if your team wins). The charity may send press releases, so if you do win the event, try to be sure your restaurant is named in them.

Situation: You are a psychotherapist and are trying to get established in the community.

Option 1: Send press releases and/or proposals to the media offering to become their expert in your area and more specifically, offer to:

- Host a weekly call-in program for a radio station.
- Provide commentary on the psychological aspects of a current news story for a television station.
- Write a weekly column for a local newspaper.

Notice that two out of the three suggestions involve speaking skills and the other requires writing skills, which will work synergistically with your press releases.

Option 2: Offer to give a speech for a group that has many potential clients, such as caregivers of Alzheimer's patients, or parents of disabled children.

Situation: You sell gardening supplies and want to get more customers into your store in late summer/early fall, when sales have traditionally been slow.

Option 1: Have a contest for the person who grows the best (or biggest) fruit or vegetable. Send press releases to newspapers and television stations to announce the contest (they'll love the visual possibilities) before it happens. Be sure to send copies of the release to any gardening groups in the area.

Depending on the tone of your contest, prizes can be anything from small trophies to merchandise gift certificates to novelty items. Give a brief speech at the opening of the event and have your employees prepared and trained to show attendees the displays you have set up promoting fall gardening needs. Follow up with another press release (with photos) to any local reporter or television station that did not attend.

Option 2: Offer to do a talk/demonstration of fall gardening activities for a local service club. Be sure the club sends out a press release before the event or offer to do it yourself.

Situation: You are opening a new bookstore and want to attract customers.

Option 1: Hold book signings. Start with local authors (who will often bring in their family, friends, and neighbors as well as interested readers). While you do the pre-event publicity, such as sending press releases to the media, don't forget to write your speech to introduce the writer. It should be brief as the writer will do most of the speaking. You can make the book signing a demonstration as well as a speech or reading if you include cookbook and craftbook authors.

Option 2: Offer a weekly story hour for children. Along with the usual press releases, call local daycare centers and offer to send them "tickets," which you can make and photocopy yourself, for the children.

Another Option: Call local schools and offer to display books written by students in a case or wall display (this will bring in the students and their families). Also, contact the press, which may give you good coverage in the local media.

Situation: You are trying to establish yourself as an expert in your subject on a national scale, but you are on a very tight budget.

Option 1: Go on-line with a computer service, such as CompuServe, America On-Line, or Prodigy, and spend time reading messages in forums that focus on topics in which you are an expert. Answer other people's questions as a service, but always include your business name in your signature footer. Keep a file of your correspondence and the results you hear from people who have used your advice. The correspondence will serve as a ready source of examples for the articles and books you write. Be sure to get the people's permission to use their stories before you use them in your writing.

Option 2: Keep an eye out for breaking news stories in which the media might be interested in commentary from someone with your expertise. Be ready to write and fax press releases the same day telling the media what you have to offer them as an interview subject.

Incorporate Your Other Talents

As you are thinking about the ways you can pull together different ideas to create a successful promotion, keep your personal skills/hobbies in mind. They might just add the sparkle you need to gain the attention you want.

Don McCulley, who was mentioned in Chapter 9, performs magic tricks as a hobby. One way he promotes himself and the manufacturers he sells for is to go to trade shows and do small magic tricks that are best viewed by groups that can gather around an exhibit. Once people have enjoyed a few minutes of his wonderful magic tricks, they are ready to hear about the advantages of the products.

What talents do you have aside from your professional skills? Are you good with a video camera? Can you do beautiful calligraphy? Can you sing up a storm? Keep these other talents in mind when you are planning promotional activities and think about ways you can integrate them with the other elements.

Starting Your Planning

Using the situations described earlier in this chapter as inspiration, start thinking about what promotional elements you could combine to help build your business.

TYPE OF EVENT
PROMOTIONAL ELEMENTS I PLAN TO USE

Type of event: _____

_____

Promotional Elements I Plan to Use: _____

_____

_____

_____

Type of event: _____

_____

Promotional Elements I Plan to Use: _____

_____

_____

_____

Type of event: _____

_____

Promotional Elements I Plan to Use: _____

_____

_____

_____

DEVELOPING A CALENDAR OF EVENTS FOR MAXIMUM EFFECTIVENESS

As you can see from the earlier examples, promotional activities don't just happen, they take thought and planning. You will need to take a little time to create a schedule of events that will best promote your business. Then you will need to take some time to work out a schedule of how you plan to achieve your goals.

You will want to have some variety in the types of promotional activities you do. Variety is important because even the most wonderful things can get boring if you do them repeatedly. After all, even riding a roller coaster at an amusement park is more exciting the first time you do it than it is the sixth time you do it the same day.

In addition, by having variety in the types of activities you do, you will reach out to a larger pool of potential customers and clients. There may be some overlap, but usually the people who find out about your business because of your involvement with a professional organization are not going to be the same people who discover your business because of your on-line computer activities or your speeches.

Getting the Timing Right

You should also consider the timing of your activities. How can you schedule them to take advantage of slow periods you expect in your business? Have you spaced them out so that they happen at different times of the year?

As you think about the activities you want to plan, make sure you have enough lead time to make them happen. Some activities, like establishing yourself on-line as an expert by answering questions and giving comments in forums, are quite spontaneous and the only planning you might need is deciding what time of the day you will go on-line. Other activities, like writing a book, may take over a year to accomplish. Most activities will fall somewhere in between.

Try to plan for activities that will require different levels of commitment of your time and energy to help keep it fun for you.

Break it down so you can see how it works. Here are some suggestions. No one can do all of them, but pick a few that interest you and make up your own sample schedule.

Sample Schedule

Daily or weekly: Check on-line forums and e-mail, read a newspaper (or watch a news program) to scout for stories you are qualified to give commentary on and send press releases to the appropriate media, observe employees to be sure they are interacting well with customers/clients, examine business site for cleanliness and neatness so it gives new customers a good impression, make one to five public-relations oriented telephone calls per week.

Monthly: Attend meetings of professional and/or business organizations, review material on your Web page for accuracy and timeliness, send out one newsworthy press release per month.

Quarterly: Plan an event that will enable you to interact with the media and your customers, review your promotional activities for the last quarter and determine which ones achieved the best results and why.

Annually: Set up a schedule of events for the coming year.

Planning Successful Events

Planning your events is much more involved than just deciding to do them. You must develop a plan that covers all the tasks that must be done, the supplies that must be acquired, the publicity that will be generated, and any other aspects that will be necessary to carry off this event successfully.

Here is a partial listing of some of the preparations you may need to make depending on the type of promotional activity you are planning:

Pre-Event Publicity
- Write and send press releases
- Follow up with press to answer any questions they have
- Hire a photographer to take pictures
- Mail invitations to guests or attendees

Pre-Event Planning
- Plan a schedule of events
- Be sure you have enough support staff
- Write a brief speech to give as an opener
- Write brief introductions for other participants/presenters
- Set up and practice any demonstrations to be sure they will work
- Set up a sign-in system or door prize drawing as a way of getting names and addresses of attendees for post-event mailing

List of Necessary Items
- Materials for demonstrations
- Samples for distributing
- Brochures/fliers for attendees to take home
- Microphone if anticipate a crowd of over twenty
- Lectern, overhead projectors, other necessary presentation equipment
- Special lighting, if needed
- Other electrical connections that may be needed

Eat, Drink, and Be Merry
- Hire a caterer and choose a menu
- Hire a bartender or beverage server
- Buy food and beverages if not using caterer
- Buy glasses, napkins, plates
- Get large trash cans and plan strategic placement
- Have adequate rest rooms available or rent portable ones

Follow-up Activities

- Have people available to clean up the site
- Send thank-you notes to people who helped
- Send press releases about your success to print media
- Send brochures/fliers to those who attended (consider including discount coupon)

SELF-SURVEY: WORKSHEETS FOR PLANNING EVENTS

Sample Schedule of Events

Daily: _____

Weekly: _____

Monthly: _____

Quarterly: _____

Annually: _____

Event Planning Sheet

Type of event: _____

Title of event: _____

Date and time: _____

Principal people involved and their role: _____

_____

_____

_____

Time line: _____

Three months ahead: _____

Two months ahead: _____

One month ahead: _____

Two weeks ahead: _____

One week ahead: _____

Three days ahead: _____

Two days ahead: _____

Event day: _____

Day after event: _____

EVENT MEDIA TRACKING RECORD

Name of Event: _____

Media Name	Date Called	Contact Name	Address	Materials Sent

Date: _____ Place: _____

Follow-Up Effort	Their Response	Results Achieved	Notes

Event Results Record

Type of Event	Date(s)	Cost	Number of Attendees

Media Present	Sales Generated	Follow-Up Tasks	Notes
	.		

EVENT MEMO FOR NEXT TIME

Name of Event: _____

Date: _____

Place: _____

Aspects of this event that went better than expected:

_____

_____

Aspects of this event that were disappointing: _____

_____

_____

What I think I can do to change them next time: _____

_____

_____

People I worked with who I want to be sure to contact next time: _____

_____

People who offered help too late to incorporate it in this event but might be helpful next time: _____

_____

Different equipment and/or supplies I should have on hand:

_____

_____

How I should change my pre-event schedule to be more effective: _____

_____

_____

_____

Glossary

Acronym A word that is formed using the first letters of a series of words, such as ASCII (American Standard Code for Information Interchange).

Advertising specialties Items that are given to clients or potential clients to remind them of your business. They are often small inexpensive items like key chains or baseball caps that have your logo on them.

Alliteration The repetitive use of an initial sound, such as the P sound in "Peter Piper picked a peck of pickled peppers."

ASCAP The American Society of Composers, Authors, and Publishers collects and distributes royalties in the music business. ASCAP, 7920 Sunset Blvd. #300, Los Angeles, CA 90046.

ASCII The American Standard Code for Information Interchange is a standard computer code used to facilitate the interchange of information among different types of data-processing equipment.

ASJA The American Society of Journalists and Authors is a prestigious organization of professional nonfiction writers. ASJA, 1501 Broadway, Suite. 302, New York, NY 10036, (212) 997-0947.

Authors' registry The registry collects and distributes royalties on articles for writers. Contact ASJA for more information.

Barter To trade or otherwise exchange products or services without using money.

Benefit The specific, positive gain that a business hopes to achieve by performing a specific act.

Book (v.) A term used to describe the process of scheduling speakers or interview subjects for television or radio programs.

Book proposal A sales document that describes your book idea and is prepared for literary agents and publishers to interest them in publishing your book.

BOR A term used by professional speakers to refer to "back of the room" tables used for selling books, tapes, and other merchandise.

Brochure A pamphlet (usually one page—often folded) that is used to promote a business.

Browser A computer program that searches through the Internet to find specified information.

Business plan A document outlining how a business is to be set up, budgeted, and run. Often required by lending institutions when the business owner is trying to get a loan.

Chamber of Commerce An organization that focuses on promoting the business health of its community and members.

Computer A programmable machine that accepts, processes, and displays data.

Copyright The exclusive right to publish or sell the rights to a work, such as an article, book, or image (photo, drawing, and so on). This right is granted by law for a certain amount of time to the creator of the work. The copyright holder can sell or license his or her copyright.

E-mail Electronic mail, such as memos, messages, and letters, that is transmitted over a computer network.

Emoticon A coded graphic shorthand (also called "smileys") often used within e-mail messages to give emotion to the written message. The images are displayed vertically and examples include :) (smile) ;) (wink) {{}} (hug) :((sad).

Entrepreneur Someone who organizes and maintains a business, usually as the owner.

Forum An on-line assembly place where open discussion occurs on subjects relating to the topic of the forum.

Hard copy Written material printed on paper, usually refers to computer printout.

Head shot A photograph that shows only a person's head or head and shoulders. Used for publicity purposes.

Intellectual property Something created by a person or company that may be protected under law by copyright, trademark, etc.

Internet The international network of computer networks that functions as a giant global switchboard. The internet enables computers and computer networks to communicate with one another.

Links An electronic connection of Web pages that allows someone viewing one page to immediately access another page belonging to another person. Linked pages may or may not have to have the same carrier.

Local media The newspapers, magazines, shoppers, television, and radio stations that serve a discrete regional area.

Manuscript A document that has been written for publication as a book or an article.

Masthead A box or section printed in each newspaper and magazine that lists the publishers, owners, and editors and the location of the editorial office and subscription address.

Media A catchall term for television and radio stations, networks, newspapers, wire services, magazines, and other information gathering and disseminating organizations.

Netiquette The art of etiquette online. The basic good manners that people are expected to observe if they want to be respected by others on-line.

Networking Developing relationships or exchanging information with others to build business contacts and further careers.

On-line Accessible by computer using a modem.

Osteopathic A school of medicine that places special emphasis on the interrelationship of the musculoskeletal system to all other body systems.

Products Things that are created by a person or business for the purpose of offering them for sale.

Promotion The act of getting information to potential clients or customers in order to influence their attitudes and behaviors.

PSA Public Service Announcement, which is usually broadcast on radio or television to give valuable information to people. Usually done at no cost to the person or organization that supplied the material.

Publicity Any information or promotional activity that gets a business noticed by the public.

Query A letter sent to a magazine publisher proposing to write an article.

Retail The activity where businesses and individuals provide products to customers.

Seminar An educational course offered to a group of students.

Signature footer A one- to four-line entry put at the end of e-mail messages that includes the writer's name and usually some other information to help readers either identify or contact the writer.

Spamming Sending an overwhelming number of unsolicited computer messages via e-mail to one person or sending a single unsolicited e-mail message to many people.

Start-ups Companies that are relatively new at being in business.

Synergy When two or more individual items or effects work together to create a result that is more than the sum of the individual components.

Sysop A "system operator." This term refers to the person who manages a forum-type area and who is an expert at both how to use the forum and its subject matter.

Usenet A "user network." It is a system of thousands of interlinked bulletin boards that is available via the Internet and most commercial on-line services. It is like a giant bulletin board, where users post, read, and exchange messages on virtually any subject.

Virtual Term used in reference to computer activities, such as "Virtual Reality." It is the creation of an artificial reality that projects the user into 3-dimensional space.

Web page A destination on the World Wide Web where individuals and companies can post information about themselves that is available to anyone using a computer on-line.

WWW The World Wide Web is a graphical, hypertext system that links many, but not all, computers connected to the Internet.

Resources

Chapter 1

Elite Leads was founded by Sharyn Abbott in 1991. The company provides meetings where business people come on a regular basis to share contacts, give and receive guidance, and help their business develop. Franchise opportunities available. Contact Elite Leads at 1630 N. Main Street, #439, Walnut Creek, CA 94596; or call (510) 939-1801. E-mail address: sharynabbott@pcld.com.

BXI, Business Exchange International, Corp., is a barter network (sometimes called trade exchange). It functions as a bank, but the transactions are based on goods and services rather than cash. Contact BXI at 333 N. Glenoaks Boulevard, #400, Burbank, CA 91502; or call (818) 563-4966.

Margaret Clark-Mayfield is the owner of MCM Computer Services, which supplies word processing, desktop publishing, database management, and bookkeeping services to small businesses. She can be contacted at 5100-1B Clayton Road, #322, Concord, CA 94521; or call (510) 686-6258. E-mail address: MargaretCM@aol.com.

Doelle Cecaci, Diablo Valley Area Director for Business Exchange International (see BXI listing for the national address). She can be contacted at 176 Valdivia Circle, San Ramon, CA 94583; or call (510) 355-0711.

Encyclopedia of Associations, see Gale Research, Inc.

Gale Research, Inc., publishers of reference books for business. The company's publications include *Small Business Sourcebook, Encyclopedia of Associations,* and related titles. The books are updated annually to provide the most currently available information. The *Encyclopedia of Associations* is also available on CD-ROM. Call (800) 877-GALE for more information about these publications and current prices.

Sally J. Nordwall, owner of Sally J. Nordwall, CLU, Financial Advisor, is also an active member of Women's Network of Contra Costa County. Contact her at 381 Boyd Road, Pleasant Hill, CA 94523; or call (510) 938-7026.

Toni Stewart is the owner of Albe Stamp & Engraving, a source for stamps, award plaques, engraving, and interior and exterior signage. Contact Albe Stamp & Engraving at 2020 S. Combee Road, Lakeland, FL 33801; or call (941) 667-0778. Active member of the Lakeland, Florida, Chamber of Commerce.

Small Business Sourcebook, see Gale Research, Inc.

U.S. Chamber of Commerce, the world's largest business federation with 215,000 business members, plus local Chambers, trade, and professional associations. Contact the U.S. Chamber of Commerce at 1615 H Street NW, Washington, DC 20062-2000; or call (800) 638-6582; in Maryland call (800) 352-1450.

Women's Network of Contra Costa County. See Sally J. Nordwall, CLU.

Marcia Yudkin, *So You Want to Write a Book,* three-cassette audiotape set, packaged with checklists and a complete book proposal that won a contract from a major publisher. $39.95 plus $3.50 shipping. To buy the audiotape set, write P.O. Box 1310, Boston, MA 02117; or call (800) 898-3546. E-mail address: marcia@yudkin.com.

Chapter 2

Carol Jensen, owner of Jensen Business Development, which helps small businesses with their business plans, start-ups, strategic marketing, and financial analysis. To contact Carol Jensen, write 377 West King, Winona, MN 55987; or call (507) 452-0525.

Chapter 3

Alan Caruba is founder of The Boring Institute and The National Anxiety Center. The institute's available publications include *Getting Famous—How to Write a Successful News Release* and *Don't Panic—an Instant Guide to Crisis Communications,* each $5 from the Caruba Organization, Box 40, Maplewood, NJ 07040; or call (201) 763-6392.

Dave Lakhani, Boise, Idaho, Computer Clearance Center store owner. His e-mail address is 75352.1274@CompuServe.com.

Jay Conrad Levinson, author of *Guerrilla Marketing Weapons,* published by Plume, a division of Penguin Books, $9.95.

Jack "Corkie" Surrette is vice president of Marketing for Tanning Research Laboratories, Inc., the manufacturers of Hawaiian Tropic tanning products. To contact Jack Surrette, write P.O. Box 265111, Daytona Beach, FL 32126; or call (904) 677-9559.

Bev Marshall, Realtor-Associate, Re/Max, Inc., C.C. Connection, Inc. To contact Bev Marshall, write 2950 Buskirk Avenue, Suite 140, Walnut Creek, CA 94596; or call (510) 937-0114.

Chapter 5

The Associated Press Stylebook is an excellent reference book and provides an alphabetical list of words, acronyms, and expressions with their correct spellings and definitions. Published by Addison-Wesley Publishing Company, $14.

The Chicago Manual of Style is published by the University of Chicago Press. This book covers manuscript preparation, style, and so on and explains the terms often used in publishing and printing. It is used by many publishers as the authority when making editing decisions on manuscripts.

Roget's International Thesaurus is an excellent resource when you are looking for just the right word (especially to replace one that is being overused). Has synonyms, antonyms, and so on.

Gordon Burgett, Communication Unlimited. To contact Communication Unlimited for information about *Publishing to Niche Markets* (also available at bookstores) and other products to help self-publishers, write P.O. Box 6405, Santa Maria, CA 93456; or call (805) 937-8711; or fax (805) 937-3035.

Tom and Marilyn Ross are owners of About Books, Inc., a writing, publishing, and marketing consulting service. The new, revised third edition of *The Complete Guide to Self-Publishing* (also available at bookstores) is available for $18.99 + $3.00 shipping from Communication Creativity, Box 909-NRL, Buena Vista, CO 81211; or call (800) 331-8355 for credit card orders.

Chapter 6

Isadora Alman, MFCC, is a board-certified sexologist specializing in communication and relationship issues. She appears on television and radio programs and has written three books: *Sex Information, May I Help You,* and *Ask Isadora.* She can be reached at 3145 Geary Boulevard, #153, San Francisco, CA 94118 or check out her Web page at www.askisadora.com.

Hans G. Rohl is with Klein & Barenblat, a legal firm specializing in property tax appeals. He can be reached at 504 Milam Building, San Antonio, TX 78205; or call (210) 227-8392.

Toastmasters International is an international (54 countries) organization that helps people improve their communication and leadership skills. To find a club near you, call (714) 858-8255 or write Toastmasters at P.O. Box 9052, Mission Viejo, CA 92690-7052 or e-mail the organization at drex@kaiwan.com. Be sure to ask about local meetings.

Lilly Walters, author and speaker consultant, owns Walters International Speakers Bureau and can be reached at P.O. Box 112, Glendora, CA 91740; or call (818) 335-8069; or e-mail: LillyW@aol.com.

Chapter 7

Al Bredenberg is the author of *The Small Business Guide to Internet Marketing,* an electronic book that is delivered in plain ASCII text format. It is available by e-mail or on 3.5" floppy for $8.75 plus shipping and handling. His Web page is http://www.copywriter.com/ab/ and he can be reached at ab@copywriter.com

The Learning Annex currently has programs in San Francisco, Los Angeles, San Diego, Sacramento, New York, Washington, DC, and Toronto. For more information about the organization's programs or to order a catalog, write them at 11850 Wilshire Boulevard, Suite 100, Los Angeles, CA 90025.

Howard L. Shenson, author of *How to Develop & Promote Successful Seminars & Workshops,* published by John Wiley & Sons, $24.95.

Speak and Grow Rich by Dottie Walters and Lilly Walters. To order a book write to Walters Speaker Services, P.O. Box 1120, Glendora, CA 91740; or call (818) 335-8069. The book costs $24.95 (hardback) plus shipping and handling.

Chapter 8

Abigail Albrecht, on-line researcher. To reach her, call (510) 825-6861; or e-mail: Albrecht@CIS.CompuServe.com.

Eppie Archuleta is a weaving artist who has been profiled in *National Geographic* and whose work has been shown in the Smithsonian. She can be reached at 8325 Highway 15, Capulin, CO 81124 or through e-mail at ccs@rmmi.com or you can go on-line to see her Web page at http://www.rmii.com/~ccs/index.html.

Noel Dunne, Christian Community Services, provides pilot projects to enable people in Colorado's San Luis Valley to become economically independent. He can be reached at 206 State Avenue, Alamosa, CO 81101; or call (719) 589-0190.

Lisa Steinberg, owner of LS Bridal: Affordable Headwear for the Cost-Conscious Bride, can be reached at 7434 Selby Road, Athens, OH 45701; or call (614) 593-8916; Web address is lsbridal@seorf.ohiou.edu or http://user.aol.com/lsbridal/private/lsbridal.htm.

Chapter 9

Fabled Service: Ordinary Acts, Extraordinary Outcomes, by Betsy Sanders and published by Pfeiffer & Co. is available for $19.95 (U.S.) or $25.95 (Canada) plus shipping and handling. To order, call (800) 274-4434.

Jesus CEO, by Laurie Beth Jones and published by Hyperion, $16.95 (U.S.) or $21.95 (Canada).

Don McCulley, Don McCulley & Associates, is a sales agent for hardware and building materials manufacturers. Contact him at 295 Coventry Circle, Brentwood, CA 94513; or call (510) 516-0245; fax (510) 516-7156.

Chapter 10

Don McCulley. See reference in Chapter 9.

Index